Walter J. Ciszek, SJ

TRIPLE NOVENA

*Extraordinary Experiences,
Powerful Prayer*

Edited by Marc Lindeijer, SJ,
and Rosemary Stets, OSF

THE FATHER WALTER CISZEK
PRAYER LEAGUE
2021

ISBN: 978-0-578981-47-5

The Gulag Collection
©Victims of Communism
Memorial Foundation, Washington, DC

Book design by *5sparrows.com*

IMPRIMATUR
Alfred A. Schlert, Bishop of Allentown

*"Surrender to God and He will
do everything for you."*

(CF. PSALM 37:5)

Contents

Introduction

Dear Reader,

It is a pleasure to meet you, a friend of Father Walter Ciszek, too. You may have read his bestseller *With God in Russia,* in which he describes his 24 years in the Soviet Union, or his spiritual classic *He Leadeth Me,* the story he really wanted to write, his soul's journey. You must have been as moved as we were, when you read how he experienced the workings of divine providence in Lubyanka Prison and in the Siberian work camps and cities where he tried to live and spread the Gospel.

As for us, we feel privileged that we were able to know Father Walter in a very special way. Sister Rosemary knew him as her spiritual father and friend for fifteen years, until his death in 1984. Father Marc worked seven years in Rome for his canonization cause, with access to his unpublished writings. He edited a number of them, together with John M. DeJak, in the volume *With God in America: The Spiritual Legacy of an Unlikely Jesuit* (2016), which covers the last twenty years of Father Ciszek's life. It is in the context of that cause that we met. When Father Marc was looking for additional testimonies to Walter Ciszek's sanctity, Sister Rosemary kindly sent him the notebooks with the memories she wrote after he had passed away.

So what is this book that you are holding now? It is a book that provides something more for those in need, for those still seeking Father Walter's unfailing counsel. The Father Walter Ciszek Prayer League, active since 1989, receives many requests from people who ask to be remembered in prayer for special intentions, or wish to pray for favors through the intercession of Father Walter. Like you, they have read his books, and they are grateful to receive some prayer cards from the League. However, many who write are seeking something to inspire them in time of prayer, like a novena which provides an experience of sustained reflection. Thus far, there was little available to help them. But

Walter Ciszek left us a precious document suited precisely for this purpose — his detailed plan for *He Leadeth Me* which he wrote about 1970. It contains many facts that did not make it into the book, but more importantly, it confirms with greater clarity the divine interventions he experienced in Russia and his own personal spiritual transformation.

Following that plan, this book will provide not just a single, but a triple novena. In three distinct settings: Lubyanka Prison, the work camps, and the town of Norilsk, God revealed himself as miracle-worker, giving Father Walter the grace he needed in each moment. For us, it was most touching and consoling to see that these three extraordinary experiences follow exactly the train of thought so beautifully expressed in Psalm 23, the psalm that prefaces *He Leadeth Me* and from which the book takes its title.

To expand the vision of Father Walter's experiences and provide a helpful context, we prefaced these novenas with the first introduction that he himself wrote for *He Leadeth Me*. We have given it the title "How I Did It", the answer to the question people asked him most often, namely, "How did you manage to survive?", and the title he originally intended for *He Leadeth Me*. Finally, we have added an appendix with a selection of Sister Rose-mary's memories, written between 1987 and 1992. They will reveal the person who returned to us from Russia — the man as he was — a holy priest, a sure guide, a dear friend to all who sought his acquaintance.

Father Walter was not a great author, as he himself publicly acknowledged. After 23 years in Russia, his difficulty with written English was understandable. He struggled to express his thoughts, and in writing, he often circled around an idea more than once in an effort to say what he really meant or felt about something. Like Father Daniel Flaherty, SJ, who co-authored his books, we had to edit his text, clarifying its meaning and correcting the English, yet always respectful of his thoughts and choice of words. The author of this book really is Walter Ciszek, just as he spoke in *With God in Russia* and *He Leadeth Me*. You will recognize him as you knew him; it is his voice that you will hear, his experiences that you will share.

We hope that encountering him again in the novenas will be a source of grace and consolation. May it help you to cope with life's difficult circumstances, encourage you in your trials, strengthen your faith, and teach you humble, continuous prayer that is so pleasing to God. Faith and prayer sustained Father Walter and gave him peace even during unbelievable suffering. Now that you are about to join our friend again on his journey with God in Russia, may his company and intercession bring you closer to God's love and providence which is never beyond our reach.

Marc Lindeijer, SJ
Rosemary Stets, OSF

Rev. Walter J. Ciszek, S.J.

How I Did It

CHOOSING A VOCATION

Everything that enters our life is shrouded in a certain mystery. We perceive it in things that surround us and even more so in all that transpires in our mind and soul. When we are young, we don't halt to consider seriously all that is human and divine within us. Young people face every event and act upon it with the exuberance proper of their age; to enjoy that freedom is their right and privilege. But then life, that master-teacher, opens its many doors to us and questions arise: What way to follow? Should I marry? What profession should I choose? However, those are not the most important questions. They may return later in life or never be answered at all. What does matter is understanding that I must choose, not what direction to take, but who I shall become. That is what we call "choosing a vocation". It involves a response from within our very being, which is, in fact, an expression of what we were from the beginning.

In the story of our life, including all the good and bad events that happen while we struggle along the way of our choice, our personal history unfolds. Each of us has a story to tell, once we have reached a certain age, but to grasp the mystery of our life requires two essential elements: our own actions and efforts, common to our human nature, and the divine power that motivates us to decide and act according to our inspirations. The second element is the most important. Why? The following account of a real-life story will make that clear. *With God in Russia* is my story. Now, I will try, in a simple way, to tell it again and show what God, the miracle-worker, can achieve through the ordinary actions of a person's life, if we allow Him to lead us.

THE STRUGGLE

Born in a Polish-American family in Shenandoah, Pennsylvania in 1904, I felt attracted to the priestly life from my early years. God, prayer, the Church, the sacraments, all religious services, fascinated me so much that I embraced them without questioning. But I kept my feelings to myself, not sharing them with anybody. The fear of sin and hell helped me to control to some extent my strong passions, domineering character, and tendency to independence. These inner forces could help me accomplish great and good things of course, but could also easily lead me to follow the whims of evil. Whatever chances I had to develop my intellect in school were overpowered by my misguided feelings and passionate outbursts of self-assertion. Conscience, not reason, restrained me from doing evil and moved me to give up the bad habits which I had already acquired. This mysterious interior voice was always there, censoring whatever wrong I did and demanding correction. Warned by my conscience, I intuitively understood the dangers involved in following impulses to satisfy my body and will which sought their own pleasure. My conscience never gave me a moment's rest. On the contrary, it frustrated and angered me, and made me want to fight against it. That struggle lasted for years. Alone, without anybody knowing about it, I battled with self and God. Not discouraged by repeated failed attempts to silence my conscience nor struck by remorse, I had recourse to prayer, seeking in all sincerity to quiet the voice of my conscience and construct my own way of life, which I wanted to work out so hard.

In that frame of mind, at the age of sixteen, I received permission from my parents to attend a private high school, Saints Cyril and Methodius Seminary at Orchard Lake, Michigan. But a few months before starting school, in the summer of 1921, the crisis came. My conscience disturbed me so much that life became unbearable. I was ready to do anything, no matter the consequences, just to free myself from these tormented feelings. At last, I decided not to oppose, but to obey my conscience. A total conversion followed, and with it the firm decision to become a priest. While in the seminary, a new and unexpected desire developed — to become a Jesuit and dedicate my life to studies. In 1928, I entered the Society of Jesus.

That same period saw the rise of communism as Stalin introduced his notorious collective farm system and championed militant atheism as the proper response of the proletariat to the wrongs caused by religion. The revolutionary change of industry and of the entire social structure in Russia had its repercussions throughout the world. The

Catholic Church reacted immediately to the 'red danger'. At the request of Pope Pius XI, a Russian College was opened in Rome to train priests to fight against the threat of communistic atheism. Again, I sensed an urgent voice within me, demanding that I dedicate myself to the Russian apostolate.

THE DECISION

From the very beginning I realized that the work I looked forward to would be one of prayer and sacrifice. I never once thought that communism would be able to defeat or discredit the inner life of the Church. Atheism was a moral crisis in people who denied God. Only grace could disperse the darkness that had befallen them, blinded as they were by their opposition to revealed truth. Prayer and sacrifice were needed. Not a prayer based on some ascetical method, but a prayer that spontaneously sprang from deep within me and made me conscious of God's presence in what I or others did, or in the things that simply happened. Even more than an awareness, it was a personal experience of God in all things. My humble belief in God communicating with me affected in some vague but perceptible way my spirit, making it fit and ready to communicate to others the God dwelling within me. How this came about never preoccupied me — that was God's business, not mine. But I felt compelled to live with God constantly, regardless of the situation or the consequences, ever ready to act according to his will. This is what guided my relationship with the Russian people.

Faith was my life's principle; it always made me God-conscious. My decision to enter Russia was decisive, but not only did I find myself totally unprepared for apostolic work in a country opposed to all forms of religion, I was also unqualified for skilled labor to make a living. My formation as a Jesuit priest had not prepared me for that. The thought of being young and inexperienced tempered for a moment the enthusiasm that initially had set me on fire to work for souls in a strange country. But instead of getting discouraged and start doubting my decision, I had recourse to faith in prayer. As always, the direction I sought came after I had contacted God and talked it over with Him. My decision demanded a readiness to do ordinary work as it came, and not be excessively disturbed by thoughts about the future. I told myself that God had given me good health, physical strength, and sufficient brains to cope with anything that might happen. Why be worried about the future? Forget it. What was supposed to happen would come anyway. Faith made me conscious that I was ready and able to handle whatever came along, even though I lacked a proper preparation. The different phases of my life in the Soviet Union ultimately served one purpose — namely, to test and increase my faith in God. A vocation, or more accurately a calling, is a life of trials. After we have been sufficiently tested by God, He, the Almighty, confirms us in grace.

THE TEST

I entered Russia on March 15, 1940. The first year and a half introduced me to the harsh reality of communism. This affected my faith, since faith is a quality of the soul, a condition touched by concrete situations where you live, work, and engage with others. I had grown up and entered religious life in America. When I went to Rome for my priestly formation in 1934 and then, four years later, to Poland for my first ministry, I had immediately been struck by the difference of life in these countries. Hence, the physical conditions of life in Russia did not trouble me so much. I had always been able to manage circumstances as they came, no matter how exceptional. It was the ideology, though, that caused me the most concern. The spirit of atheism was everywhere and pervaded everything, at work, at home, at the movies, in clubhouses, in libraries. How could people be so easily influenced by crude propaganda? At the same time, what chance did I, a priest, have against the all-powerful soviet state to spread religion amongst its citizens? None at all. The seeming futility of my mission discouraged and frustrated me, and it would continue to oppress me during the entire 23 years that I remained in Russia. Inexperienced as I was in the spiritual life, I tried to control these feelings. I thought that my will sufficed to subdue my feelings of fear and insecurity. But soon I learned that self-control, no matter how sincere and well-intended, made these feelings only stronger. The growing tension took away my peace and left me even more depressed. Faith was needed, otherwise my whole mission would fail.

Then suddenly things changed. On June 22, 1941, the day Germany invaded Russia, I was arrested and five years of solitary confinement in Moscow's Lubianka prison followed. Instead of the apostolate among the workers that I had planned, I faced a seemingly endless trial, along with hunger, cold, and a strict prison regime. Already preoccupied with all kinds of fears, especially the fear of losing faith in God, I was further tormented by a deep feeling of abandonment. The situation was aggravated by the mistakes I made during the interrogations, and the cooperation the interrogator forced upon me. To refuse cooperation meant immediate execution, as soviet law demanded for foreign spies. Why believe in a God, a Church they asked, when the atheistic Soviet Union demonstrated to all the world that one could build a new society without the help of God, religion, or priests? My interrogator talked as any communist would, rejecting the supernatural. I was forced to listen to such talk against all that faith brought me, yet I kept on believing, in spite of my inability to argue it out with him. How come? Because I stuck close to the life of faith deep within me, respecting and following it not as the interrogator imagined, but as I knew it to be. For this I paid heavily.

I prayed long hours every day, but God's presence seemed distant to me, a dream, an illusion of the past. The absolute silence of God in those five years of unrelenting trial nearly made me want to surrender to the pressure of the interrogator and let happen what may. However, this idea did not fit my spiritual way of thinking. Instead of giving in, I turned to prayer and persevered until that dangerous thought disappeared. After five years in prison, I refused to sign the paper they handed me, a refusal that cost me ten years of hard labor in Siberia. But in the end, I was even ready for that experience. First of all, those years of solitary confinement provided me with a deep spirit of prayer. They also gave me courage and trust in God, even when my conscience was troubled and tortured by guilt. They gave me a deeper appreciation of grace, how much it meant to me in situations where I felt worthless and guilty for wasting what had been entrusted to me — a feeling prompted by memories of my sins from the past. Finally, those five years gave me a noticeable increase in faith.

The camps in Siberia, first Dudinka and then in December 1946 Norilsk, had their own hardships to offer. After five years of inactivity, I had to work as a slave, without proper food or clothing, and suffer severe cold. But I was able to share these hardships with other victims which was a definite advantage in every respect, especially after all those years of loneliness. Moreover, although fully engaged in physical work, my real interest was very different — my own spiritual life and that of others. While I was in prison, and now working in the cold tundra, I yearned with all my heart to share my spiritual insights with others; I was convinced that it would benefit and comfort them. I felt at ease and free to engage them in spiritual conversations. I did not force people to talk about God, religion or spirituality; such topics arose spontaneously in the course of conversation. I always spent the evenings after work in the company of my fellow prisoners who, most of the time, came freely to me to talk things over. These friendly conversations rarely ended without some spiritual profit.

The continuous apostolic work, with frequent secret celebrations of the Eucharist and the sacrament of penance, kept me enthusiastic. The camp life was hard and the manual work exhausting, but it never depressed or discouraged me. My zeal, like a burning flame, set me afire for souls in need, not only in spiritual encounters, but also when working alone in the snowbound and cracking-cold atmosphere of the North. The thought of being helpful to others who really suffered, physically and spiritually, and for whom nobody seemed to care, brought me immense joy. I could hardly contain my thanks to God for the benefits He lavished on these abandoned prisoners who were considered outcasts of society and treated as such. God really did care for his children, no matter where they were, no matter what their condition. He reminded them in so many ways to remember what they owed Him in return. This was his command, his holy will. The prisoners who believed in God and now found themselves in this most trying situation, had no choice but to humbly bow down before their Creator and accept the suffering He sent them. By doing so, they were filled with his power; this changed their whole outlook for the future and made them less concerned about how and when their life in the camps would end.

The end of my prison term, in April 1955, did not end my trials. Leaving the camps was the beginning of my real apostolate. I had to work for a living, but that was only an occupation; my heart was wholly involved with the priestly ministry: daily Mass, services for the dead, funerals, sick calls, baptisms, marriages. The underground parish became my mission to which I dedicated myself entirely. Even though the soviet constitution allowed freedom of conscience, spreading religion openly was against the law, and the least transgression would incur immediate punishment. So I had to proceed cautiously, taking advantage of every occasion that presented itself to proclaim Christ against the false promises of atheism. The watchful eyes and the constant threats of the secret police followed me everywhere, but that did not deter me from continuing my work. They even exiled me twice, first from Norilsk, and then, in 1958, from Krasnoyarsk to Abakan in South-East Siberia. There, the police checked on me regularly, so I had to diminish my apostolic activity considerably and live as the rest of the soviet citizens, working and fulfilling state plans. But that wasn't enough for me; I never forgot I was a priest. Some women even wanted to marry me, causing me considerable trouble, yet neither marriage nor communism ever attracted me. That was not what I wanted in life. God saw my sincerity and never abandoned me. When I was tempted most, He intervened. Really, no human power in the world can equal the power of God. So I returned to my own country on October 12, 1963 as divine providence had decided, giving me the opportunity to enjoy freedom again and to contemplate and praise the goodness of God, to whom I am eternally obliged as long as I live.

FAITH AND PRAYER

In the long years of persecution that I suffered in the Soviet Union, I developed a rule of life adapted to the circumstances. Primarily, it consisted of continuous prayer and humble faith in God. This faith put God first, above all that happened, good or bad. This faith thrived in suffering and adversity; it helped me believe in God as all-knowing, all-powerful, all-merciful, and good, even when I felt no peace or consolation. This faith trusted in God, in spite of total failure and personal sin.

Faith for me was an essential part of human life as such. It did not need any theological explanation; the reality of its presence in my soul sufficed to convince my mind of its power. Faith gave me an access to God, the ability to accept Him as He revealed himself to my interior vision and made me sensitive to his continuous inspirations and promptings to action. When I entered Russia, I knew from the start that God had entrusted me with a mission, and its success depended totally on grace, not on my effort. Our humanity—mind, body, will—simply exists; it does not in any way influence grace, increase or decrease its power. Faith, in this life, is the intuitive knowledge infused by God which makes the soul ready to react properly to God's promptings. In a word, the mysterious power of the mysterious Being operating within us creates a mysterious effect on our whole life in faith, through faith, and by faith. Living faith is the only fair answer one can give to explain in some infinitesimal way how the workings of grace impact our human nature.

For me, in my long years of suffering in Russia, faith was an intense experience of God, of being with Him, especially in moments when the realization of my weakness became overwhelming and the pressure of daily misery, human contempt, and state oppression was almost impossible to bear. During that time, long periods of spiritual darkness left my soul and mind deprived of peace and caused me to feel apathy toward all that was supernatural or natural. Why bother at all, I asked myself. Who cares? People? Only for themselves. Who understands? God? Where is He? Sometimes I felt so lonely that I began to question my stand on religion and on God. Would the circumstances not justify compromising my spiritual principles and become like the rest of the people in this 'new society'? Yet even in such moments of depression and distress, my soul was never deprived of hope. Its rays, like the sun in the morning, brought about a slow change within and restored the reality of God's unchanging presence, just as the dispersing clouds reveal the radiant sun. The normal course of human life passes through such cycles repeatedly, obscuring and damping the vision of God to a considerable degree but never blocking it out entirely, not even in case of serious sin. Suffering patiently those dilemmas and persevering in prayer was exactly what I needed to discover that loneliness was the grace given to me at that moment. It was precisely what God wanted from me: to sense deeply the pains of loneliness, confusion, and guilt, and to accept them in a spirit of faith and serve God without change or compromise.

Even when the night of the soul is pitch dark, there are forces at work in heaven, in God himself, which restore the light of grace to the sinner. I constantly contemplated the misery that afflicted me, but also the suffering of the people around me who were deprived of faith and religion. I felt deep sympathy for them. Saving grace somehow touched these people, as it did all human beings in the world. This I knew and believed, convinced as I was that God knew what He was doing in all that happened to me and to them. My view of salvation, my own and that of each person, became one of absolute trust in God; my apostolic life became one of humble prayer, supported by the sacrifices demanded from me day after day. Prayer, in fact, is the main concern of the true apostle. But not only his; all Christians are called to serve God in that way. Prayer lifts you up to the level of grace; it gives a divine touch to everything you do. As a priest and religious, I had bound myself to a life of prayer. Any serious negligence on my part would have a negative effect on my apostolic work. My main task, deeply felt, was to search for God and bring Him to others, in the way grace enlightened me. But before I could convert others, I had to convert myself — a self-conversion beginning with prayer and never ending. The light of grace made me see the need for purification, and faith showed me clearly that this purification consisted in begging God's mercy, trustfully fearing Him, and being ready to do whatever his holy will proposed.

Throughout the long years in Russia, I developed a deep and conscious awareness of the workings of grace. Sensitive to its presence, I was ready and responsive to these God-given inspirations in my soul. Leading a life of prayer, I experienced its spiritual benefits; it also enabled me to touch people's souls and to help them find God themselves — a work totally belonging to the Holy Spirit. When I witnessed such a miracle of grace happening in someone else's soul, it touched and humbled me deeply. I considered those who came to me for help as sent by God and served them as my mission, my apostolic work. I had no doubt that God's favor descended on such people, but to help them on my own strength and try to convert them with no certainty that this is what God wanted, seemed as futile as it was presumptuous. However, I was deeply convinced that God would direct my work and provide opportunities when my assistance was needed, and so He did. So many people turned to me for spiritual help that at times it seemed impossible to meet all their needs. Yet I remained dedicated to them wholeheartedly and acted upon it with unrestrained self-sacrifice. Those who give themselves wholly to God's service understand well what this self-sacrifice means. The generosity of a person touched by grace knows no limits. And God, who knows all, and provides all, can make all things be well.

Novena I

IN TIMES OF FEAR AND ANXIETY

The Lord is my shepherd;
there is nothing I lack.

In green pastures he makes me
lie down; to still waters he
leads me; he restores my soul.

He guides me along right paths for
the sake of his name.

—PSALM 23:1-3

In the NKVD's Dungeon
by Nikolai Getman.
See page 137 for more
information.

DAY ONE

Reduced to Nothing

Daily Offering (see page 87)

The secret police arrested me and many others on June 22, 1941, the day Germany invaded Russia. I had been living as a good soviet citizen, so the arrest bewildered me. It was impossible, however, to argue or plead innocence; the police had their orders and that was it. Helplessness is the only word to describe my experience. It was the total loss of my freedom and the sense of being totally controlled in every action or need by someone else.

Once imprisoned in Perm, I learned the charge made against me: I was considered a Vatican spy. The interrogators used every form of physical and psychological pressure to make me admit my guilt, including beatings with rubber clubs and isolation in a cramped, dark cell to "refresh my memory". Their treatment was cruel, brutal, and degrading. Some prisoners just stopped believing they were human. There was nowhere to turn for help; indeed, every protest was considered a new transgression, a new offense against the regime.

The ordeal lasted for three months. Finally I was summoned to Moscow. During this ordeal, I could not believe that men could be as cruel to each other as the interrogators were toward the prisoners. They showed no compassion for their victims. But my misery intensified when the political prisoners discovered that I was a priest. In the eyes of both prisoners and prison officials alike, I was without value. I was totally worthless and the object of their mutual hatred.

℣. *The souls of the righteous are in the hand of God, and no torment shall touch them.*

℞. *As gold in the furnace, he proved them, and as sacrificial offerings he took them to himself.*

Our Father …

Five Hail Mary's, in honor of the years that Walter Ciszek spent in prison

Glory be …

Intercessory Prayer (see page 87)

DAY TWO
Prayer

Daily Offering (see page 87)

Lubyanka Prison, Moscow, had formerly been a hotel. The cells were small, neat, and very clean, with a wooden floor and whitewashed walls. They had one window, but barred and covered over with a sheet of tin; the only thing I could see was a little bit of the sky. Time was punctuated by the big clock in the nearby Kremlin.

I spent five years in Lubyanka — alone, isolated, hungry, cold, unwanted, considered an enemy of the people, a spy. To ward off excessive fear and the risk of losing my faith, I turned to prayer. I made up a "daily order" for myself. As soon as we were awakened, I would say the Morning Offering. Then, after the wash-up, I would dedicate a solid hour to meditation. After breakfast, I would pray the Mass by heart — that is, I would say the prayers, for there was no possibility of actually celebrating the Eucharist. I said the Angelus morning, noon, and night, as the Kremlin clock tolled. At noon and before going to bed at night, I would make an examen of conscience, a daily Jesuit practice. Each afternoon, I said three rosaries, in three different languages, as a substitute for my breviary.

In spite of these efforts, my prayer was continually distracted by constant pangs of hunger, by anxiety in not knowing when the trial would end, and by fear that I might succumb to the proposal of the interrogators — to leave the priesthood and join their ranks, "for the good of the people".

℣. *The souls of the righteous are in the hand of God, and no torment shall touch them.*

℟. *As gold in the furnace, he proved them, and as sacrificial offerings he took them to himself.*

Our Father …

Five Hail Mary's, in honor of the years that Walter Ciszek spent in prison

Glory be …

Intercessory Prayer (see page 87)

DAY THREE
Brought to Trial

Daily Offering (see page 87)

When I was first summoned for interrogation, I felt completely at ease and confident. The charge of being a Vatican spy was just too absurd. However, my interrogators hammered away in deadly earnest to get me to admit to it. Sessions might last for days at a time, with a number of interrogators who employed a variety of tactics, always with the same goal. I tried to argue about the incongruence of their accusations, but in the end, I simply had to give up.

During the long months of interrogations, my optimism and self-confidence gradually began to fade. I grew tired of fighting and ever more anxious about the prolonged years of trial. With my self-control failing, I tried to deepen my devotion to God the Father, and surprisingly, the assurance of his providential care seemed strong as ever. Not once did I feel inclined to accept the proposals the interrogators pressed upon me. Something within me always prompted me to turn to God before making any decision; the fear, resentment, and caution I felt during the sessions were always mingled with prayer. No matter what happened to me during those days and years in prison, I never failed to bring it before God and align it somehow with his will.

Finally, the day came when my strength weakened beyond what I could endure. The last interrogator, a clever manipulator, deceitfully tricked me into "telling the truth". Once I had given in that much there was no return. Fear took control and prayer didn't support me anymore — I signed their dossier. The verdict was fifteen years of hard labor in Siberia.

℣. *The souls of the righteous are in the hand of God, and no torment shall touch them.*

℞. *As gold in the furnace, he proved them, and as sacrificial offerings he took them to himself.*

Our Father …

Five Hail Mary's, in honor of the years that Walter Ciszek spent in prison

Glory be …

Intercessory Prayer (see page 87)

DAY FOUR
Abandoned by God

Daily Offering (see page 87)

The thought of being sent to the work camp, of being with people again, lifted my spirit and filled me with great joy. One year in isolation was more than enough for any man to bear. But when four more years dragged on without deportation, I became deeply disillusioned. Even when I thought my faith had been tested enough, God had to purge me of dependence upon self and lead me to rely on Him alone.

Since signing the dossier meant I had agreed to collaborate, the interrogator assumed that the next sessions to "clarify" things would be more productive. For my part, I felt terribly afraid, trapped by the interrogator, alone in prison, seemingly abandoned by God. Even prayer seemed impossible. Having failed once, I feared I would fail again, and this time lose the last thing I still clung to, my faith in God. I kept hoping that God would intervene in some miraculous way, but that did not happen.

Again, the interrogator proposed that I actively work as a communist spy or an Orthodox priest for the communist government. I wanted to say no but could not, and so I began to rely on my formation as a priest to prolong the argument and postpone a decision. But the interrogator proved to be more capable. By making mistakes in my answers, I seemed to incriminate others and betray the Church and its teachings. While trying to justify myself, my sense of guilt increased to the point of despair. These thoughts passed in a moment, but their lasting effects transformed my whole spirituality.

℣. *The souls of the righteous are in the hand of God, and no torment shall touch them.*

℟. *As gold in the furnace, he proved them, and as sacrificial offerings he took them to himself.*

Our Father ...

Five Hail Mary's, in honor of the years that Walter Ciszek spent in prison

Glory be ...

Intercessory Prayer (see page 87)

DAY FIVE
Despair

Daily Offering (see page 87)

The turning point came after nearly two years of "clarifications". Throughout this ordeal, I continued to persevere in prayer, but I also relied on self by my constant human effort, as if the solution to my problems depended entirely on me. I continued to be troubled and indecisive, not knowing whether to collaborate with the officials or not. And yet I knew that every time I failed to make a decision, the harder it would be to ultimately take a firm stand. Prayers helped, but did not take away the doubts I had.

Then one day the blackness closed in around me completely. I was exhausted by the relentless questioning, and I knew I could not postpone much longer the decision that confronted me. I despaired in the most literal sense of the word, seeing only my own weakness and helplessness. It wasn't fear of the camps or fear of death that troubled me; in fact, I sometimes thought of death by suicide as the only way out of this dilemma. No, what brought me to despair was the hopelessness of it all and my powerlessness to cope with it.

I don't know how long that dark moment lasted, but when it passed I was horrified and bewildered. In that one moment of blackness, I had not only lost hope, but lost the last shreds of my faith in God. I had stood alone in a void, separated from the One who had been my constant guide and source of consolation in all my other failures.

℣. *The souls of the righteous are in the hand of God, and no torment shall touch them.*

℟. *As gold in the furnace, he proved them, and as sacrificial offerings he took them to himself.*

Our Father …

Five Hail Mary's, in honor of the years that Walter Ciszek spent in prison

Glory be …

Intercessory Prayer (see page 87)

DAY SIX
Interior Conversion

Daily Offering (see page 87)

Everything that preceded this moment, all the events and actions of the preceding years, ultimately led to this crisis. Standing on the brink of total darkness, I desperately turned to God in prayer. This conversion moment created a fundamental change in my spiritual life. It did not impede my will or mind, but redirected everything to God; from this source flowed all the inspiration, motivation, and strength to act.

I had been trying to use my own will and mind to do something that was beyond my capabilities and basically all wrong. God's will was not hidden "out there" in mysteries I could not understand. The real and immediate situations of each day were God's will for me. Every moment of life, with all its good and bad, reflects God himself. I recognized Him in the most concrete and common things around me, revealing his will for me to follow. This new relationship with God fascinated and fulfilled me. Faith made it real and true as nothing else ever had before. I found God present in creation, ever communicating and responding to faith's quest, the center of life and existence, encompassing past, present, and future.

The realization of God's immensity filled my heart with a sense of inner dignity. The mystery remained impenetrable, yet it affected my soul deeply and made me conscious of God's indwelling. Gradually, my mind began to participate in this experience too, in its own limited way. I even felt a physical sense of belonging to God.

℣. *The souls of the righteous are in the hand of God, and no torment shall touch them.*

℟. *As gold in the furnace, he proved them, and as sacrificial offerings he took them to himself.*

Our Father …

Five Hail Mary's, in honor of the years that Walter Ciszek spent in prison

Glory be …

Intercessory Prayer (see page 87)

DAY SEVEN
God's Will Alone

Daily Offering (see page 87)

Why had it taken me so long to learn this truth? God wanted me to accept my life with its good and bad as coming from his hands, and to place myself entirely at his disposal. What He was asking of me was an act of total trust, of absolute faith in his providence. I needed an experience of complete despair, seeing my own powers and abilities fail me, before I could bring myself to make this perfect act of faith.

That moment of darkness, that experience of despair completely changed me. I can't explain how one experience could have such an immediate and lasting effect on my spiritual life, especially when so many other experiences and graces had no such effect. From that moment on, consciously and willingly, I chose to abandon myself to God's will as seen in the circumstances of every day. It was a true conversion, a gift from God which I freely and gratefully accepted without question or hesitation.

Suddenly, things seemed so simple. There was but a single vision, seeing God who was all, in all. His will, and his will alone, directed all things, and I had only to discern it in every situation and circumstance in which I found myself. The past with all its failures was not forgotten; it remained to remind me of my weakness and my misguided self-reliance. From now on however, I would rely only on God, with confidence and joy.

℣. *The souls of the righteous are in the hand of God, and no torment shall touch them.*

℟. *As gold in the furnace, he proved them, and as sacrificial offerings he took them to himself.*

Our Father …

Five Hail Mary's, in honor of the years that Walter Ciszek spent in prison

Glory be …

Intercessory Prayer (see page 87)

DAY EIGHT
Secure in His Grace

Daily Offering (see page 87)

Until that moment of despair and conversion, I had been undecided about either giving my consent to my interrogator, or refusing his proposal to work for the communist regime. It was now Spring 1944, and I was in my third year as a Lubyanka prisoner. Until now, neither willpower nor prayer had been enough to dispel my doubts. But finally, with this spiritual transformation, my whole attitude changed.

I no longer dreaded the next interview with the interrogator. All things came from God, so why should I fear them? How could I make a "mistake", when God's will was behind every development and every alternative? Secure in his grace, I felt capable of facing every situation and meeting every challenge; whatever God chose to send me in the future, I would accept.

The change in me was so striking that even the interrogator noticed it. His newest proposal was that I might serve as chaplain in one of the newly formed Polish armies that fought together with the Russian troops. Totally relaxed, I told him that I was willing to agree. His reaction was one of surprise — pleased, but also a bit suspicious of my sudden change of heart. He told me he would report to his superiors and let me know their answer as soon as he heard. No longer troubled by fear and doubts, it was clear to me now what to do when the interrogator would summon me to sign the paper.

℣. *The souls of the righteous are in the hand of God, and no torment shall touch them.*

℟. *As gold in the furnace, he proved them, and as sacrificial offerings he took them to himself.*

Our Father …

Five Hail Mary's, in honor of the years that Walter Ciszek spent in prison

Glory be …

Intercessory Prayer (see page 87)

DAY NINE
The Decision

Daily Offering (see page 87)

The next time I saw the interrogator, he presented the new proposal. The sessions continued as before, but I remained perfectly relaxed. If these things were to be, then they had a purpose known to God alone. If they were not to be, then they would never happen. My confidence in his providence was absolute. I only had to follow the promptings of his grace. When a moment of decision came, He would lead me on the right path.

And so it happened. When at last the interrogator handed me the paper to sign, I pushed it aside and said that I refused to work as their agent. I had not planned it; I had simply gone along with everything up to that point. But suddenly it seemed the right thing to do, and I did it. Furious about my refusal, the interrogator sent me away, not to my cell but to an isolation room in the basement. Accompanied by the guards, I felt as if guided by angels towards a future of God's making.

My change of attitude had made it easy to make the decision I had dreaded so much. It taught me that grace is given in its proper time, as God sees fit. No sooner, no later. Until then, we must persevere in faith, patience, and prayer; that is the conformity to his will required from us. My refusal to collaborate would bring me to Siberia, and there again, I would find God at my side.

℣. *The souls of the righteous are in the hand of God, and no torment shall touch them.*

℞. *As gold in the furnace, he proved them, and as sacrificial offerings he took them to himself.*

Our Father …

Five Hail Mary's, in honor of the years that Walter Ciszek spent in prison

Glory be …

Intercessory Prayer (see page 87)

Waiting to be Shot by Nikolai Getman
See page 138 for more information.

Novena II

IN THE FACE OF DEATH

*Even though I walk through the
valley of the shadow of death,*

*I will fear no evil, for you are
with me;*

*your rod and your staff
comfort me.*

—PSALM 23:4

DAY ONE
Journey to the Camps

Daily Offering (see page 87)

Five years in prison seemed more than enough for me. If God wanted me to stay longer, I was ready for that. But going to the camps filled me with joy and new expectations. No matter what difficulties and hardships I might encounter in the camps, to be with people again and work with them would be most rewarding. After the five years of isolation in prison, the camps appeared to be a great grace.

The journey from Moscow to Krasnoyarsk, then to Dudinka and Norilsk in the Arctic Circle, continued to lift my spirits. I met and talked with other prisoners day and night, listening intently to their stories. I eagerly watched the passing landscape, the towns, the villages and cities, and the people on the farms we passed. At that time, I could not believe that the camps could be as terrible as some prisoners described, especially compared with my trying experience in prison.

In the past, I had always felt a certain feeling of security deep within me, but now I felt it in a new way. I believed that I was really being led by God, and more than ever, I confided in his power. If only

I could abandon myself to this unlimited power, nothing evil could befall me. This desire began to occupy my thoughts completely. In the Arctic Circle, I would soon have the opportunity to prove how sincere my desire was.

℣. *If God is for us, who can be against us?*

℟. *God did not spare his only Son, but handed him over for us all. How will He not also give us everything else along with Him?*

Our Father …

Nine Hail Mary's, in honor of the years that Walter Ciszek spent in the camps

Glory be …

Intercessory Prayer (see page 87)

DAY TWO
Hard Work

Daily Offering (see page 87)

The first test of my desire to abandon myself to God was the hard physical work of mining and construction on a permanently frozen earth. We labored long hours with primitive tools and inadequate clothing, along with constant hunger and fear adding to the burden.

It was my body that suffered most. How was it going to survive the long years of enforced labor and camp life? I had always disregarded bodily needs, but now I saw that it too was sacred, like the soul. It had to carry burdens, but it was also the vessel of God's grace, filled with holiness and the highest aspirations. This new attitude gave me the courage to bear the dirt, exhaustion, and humiliation with a spirit of resignation. Once accepted, the physical and moral hardships reflected in some unclear way the will of God, which I humbly recognized through faith.

Living with other prisoners also gave me much moral energy. Each prisoner had sufferings uniquely his own, which kept me from feeling oversensitive about my own problems. Indeed, many suffered more than I did, especially those without faith, who depended only on their own strength to survive, endure, and work out problems. It made me even more grateful for the gift of my faith, which kept me balanced and gave me hope and strength to persevere in adversity.

℣. *If God is for us, who can be against us?*

℟. *He who did not spare his own Son but handed him over for us all, how will he not also give us everything else along with him?*

Our Father …

Nine Hail Mary's, in honor of the years that Walter Ciszek spent in the camps

Glory be …

Intercessory Prayer (see page 87)

DAY THREE
Repression

Daily Offering (see page 87)

In the camps, we had no freedom or rights; we were totally dependent on the mercy of the camp officials. The food was barely enough to survive; the hard work was intended to discipline and punish us. The frequent raids and interrogations, the cruelty of camp officials and guards who treated us as social outcasts and enemies of the people — all made us feel inferior every moment of the day.

Impoverished and demoralized, the prisoners' language became obscene and their behavior vulgar; I even had to sleep with a knife to defend myself against sexual aggression. Their interactions were selfish, disrespectful, and cruel; suspicion and revenge often ended in murder. There were few tender consciences in the camp about such matters. A man did what he had to do to survive at all costs. Yet with their homes and families broken and no certainty of ever leaving the camp again, the prisoners grew discouraged, and in the end desperate.

The camp officials spread atheistic and materialistic doctrine through all possible means. They did not tolerate any opposition. Prisoners, undesirable elements, were to be "re-educated" for a new workers' paradise. Afraid of reprisals, the prisoners did not protest against communism, even though they detested it. They expressed their contempt for the camp officials who were responsible for this inhuman treatment first through subversive behavior, and finally through unrestrained revolt.

℣. *If God is for us, who can be against us?*

℟. *He who did not spare his own Son but handed him over for us all, how will he not also give us everything else along with him?*

Our Father …

Nine Hail Mary's, in honor of the years that Walter Ciszek spent in the camps

Glory be …

Intercessory Prayer (see page 87)

DAY FOUR
Revolt

Daily Offering (see page 87)

In March 1953, the news was broadcast throughout the camp that Stalin was dead. It soon led to a revolt among the prisoners, their last resort in hoping for a long awaited change. Their demands were basic human rights, to be seen and treated as human beings. Opposing or disagreeing with communism was no reason for arrest and brutal treatment. Nor should transgressions of soviet law deprive people of their human dignity. These were the common demands circulating among the prisoners protesting against the rule of force and terror.

After a few confrontations between the prisoners and the guards, all work in the camp stopped. Fear of reprisal kept the prisoners from excessive violence. Instead, they formed a committee to take control of the camp and negotiate with the camp officials. They avoided political issues, but instead, stressed the abuses in the camp and demanded that the conditions be completely remedied — no more than eight hours of work a day, better food, fair wages, and no numbers on their clothing. They also demanded permission to write letters to their families once a month instead of once a year, and to receive their visits.

The camp officials assured the prisoners that their demands would be met, but the prisoners were doubtful. As for me, I was preoccupied with the uncertain outcome of the revolt, but this did not disturb my inner peace. The decision to hold out against the officials and demand that Moscow look into the camp conditions was an act of great courage.

℣. *If God is for us, who can be against us?*

℟. *He who did not spare his own Son but handed him over for us all, how will he not also give us everything else along with him?*

Our Father …

Nine Hail Mary's, in honor of the years that Walter Ciszek spent in the camps

Glory be …

Intercessory Prayer (see page 87)

DAY FIVE
Armed Resistance

Daily Offering (see page 87)

That first evening the day of the revolt, troops came out to reinforce the camp guards and surround the prison complex. The prisoners began to organize themselves, determined not to work anymore but to fight for freedom. Next morning, I talked with a camp official near the fence. He told me the revolts in the camps were now widespread, but since Moscow had not yet decided how to react, no one was willing to use force.

A few days later, word came that the officials had promised better conditions. We were given many of the changes requested, and most of the others were promised. However, since the officials had negotiated without including the prisoners, many doubted the outcomes. The longer it took to reach a settlement, the more dissatisfied we became.

The truce did not last very long. By mid-April, troops were deployed to the camp and promises turned into threats. While the leaders of the revolt refused to be intimidated, the majority of prisoners were disheartened and refused to cooperate. When troops entered the camp five days later, they met with little resistance. We knelt behind our piles of brick, which had to serve both as shelter and weapons, but the soldiers easily overpowered us. They didn't bother to shoot; they just used their guns as clubs. I was hit across the back and leveled to the floor. Then one by one we were thrown out of the windows, like sacks of cement.

℣. *If God is for us, who can be against us?*

℟. *He who did not spare his own Son but handed him over for us all, how will he not also give us everything else along with him?*

Our Father …

Nine Hail Mary's, in honor of the years that Walter Ciszek spent in the camps

Glory be …

Intercessory Prayer (see page 87)

DAY SIX

Before the Firing Squad

Daily Offering (see page 87)

After the failed revolt, we were easily conquered, rounded up, and led in large groups into the taiga by the panicky soldiers. The sudden and sorrowful ending of the revolt made every prisoner fear for his life. I experienced a sense of failure combined with great sympathy for the dead, a deep and wounding sorrow, and extreme emotional distress. We all knew our life was at stake.

Never had I seen men so depressed and helpless as the prisoners amassed in the taiga awaiting their verdict. We had no idea what disciplinary measures would befall us, but we never for a moment thought we would be facing a firing squad. We were ordered into the clay pits, ankle deep in water, facing the soldiers lined up five yards in front of us with machine guns ready, waiting only for the command to shoot.

Like my fellow prisoners, I was paralyzed with fear. But in spite of the imminent danger, I still felt God's presence. I refrained from talking to others about God, but I noticed many were praying silently. Although all were touched similarly by the outcome of the revolt, those who turned to God at that moment felt his sure and certain help. In some vague but powerful way, they felt less hopeless and more secure. That indistinct sign of God's presence was all we could cling to. My utter helplessness and God's infinite power converged to keep me safe, and gave me a wondrous sense of God's loving concern for my personal good.

℣. *If God is for us, who can be against us?*

℟. *He who did not spare his own Son but handed him over for us all, how will he not also give us everything else along with him?*

Our Father …

Nine Hail Mary's, in honor of the years that Walter Ciszek spent in the camps

Glory be …

Intercessory Prayer (see page 87)

DAY SEVEN
Saved from Death

Daily Offering (see page 87)

Looking into the gun barrels, we knew we were a heartbeat from death. After a moment's pause, the commandant approached, gave a command, and the soldiers leveled their machine guns at us. I couldn't move a muscle in my body and my mind went blank. I thought "is this the end, Lord?" and began a feeble Act of Contrition.

Waiting for the shots seemed like an eternity. Gripped by fear in this last moment of life, I was powerless to utter a single prayer before meeting my Redeemer. Suddenly there was a shot in the distance, and a car roared to a stop in front of us. Two camp officials jumped out, shouted some orders, and the soldiers immediately lowered their guns. My heart was pounding and my knees were trembling. When we were finally ordered to sit down on the wet ground, I simply collapsed.

Later, as we began the march back to camp, I struggled to understand what had just happened. I knew my panic before the firing squad was a normal human reaction to the fear of imminent death. But not until we returned to camp did I realize the great lesson learned from this experience. It was God's providence which had intervened, manifesting his loving care for each of us — something that seemed incomprehensible. It became evident to all of us, and it strengthened our faith in God immensely. We had not been able to help ourselves in that last desperate moment. It was God alone who had worked out our salvation.

℣. *If God is for us, who can be against us?*

℟. *He who did not spare his own Son but handed him over for us all, how will he not also give us everything else along with him?*

Our Father …

Nine Hail Mary's, in honor of the years that Walter Ciszek spent in the camps

Glory be …

Intercessory Prayer (see page 87)

DAY EIGHT
The Power of Providence

Daily Offering (see page 87)

After this traumatic ordeal, I longed for some time to myself to pray, but when the truck arrived to bring us back to camp, the only thought running through my mind was "this is where we get dumped somewhere, never to be seen again." But that moment of self-pity, picturing myself lost and forgotten in a clay pit in Siberia, passed quickly. I began to reason with myself: "Do you think God doesn't know where you are? Do you think He has protected you thus far and has now just forgotten about you?" I was immediately flooded with renewed confidence in God's providence and felt my strong faith return.

It is not we who achieve our salvation; it is God's total gift. The power of this truth helped me realize that my attention should not be on myself: what I do, where I am, or on people, objects, desires and passions, sin or evil which exists everywhere. My focus is God, the center of my life, the source of all good. Everything else — spiritual, physical, material — gets its meaning from this vision of God, which mysteriously touches every soul through grace.

Life, with all its good and evil, its constant change, growth and decline, ups and downs, in a word, all that can possibly occur to us in our relation to the universe and to eternity, continues its course heavenward through that divine power called Providence. In that unfathomable power, our earthly and eternal life is firmly rooted.

℣. *If God is for us, who can be against us?*

℟. *He who did not spare his own Son but handed him over for us all, how will he not also give us everything else along with him?*

Our Father …

Nine Hail Mary's, in honor of the years that Walter Ciszek spent in the camps

Glory be …

Intercessory Prayer (see page 87)

DAY NINE
Abandonment

Daily Offering (see page 87)

Back in the camp, it was a long time before I was able to sleep. Even after the others had left, I relived the experience of the afternoon over and over again, realizing how it might have turned out, and thanking God for the actual outcome.

My faith in Him was not in any way my achievement, but his pure gift. It was up to me to accept God's providence with all its demands. Whatever I do, sense, think or desire, I must discern the presence and working of that divine power in human life as well as in nature. This conscious, spiritual way of seeing God's providence at work in my life is the only thing that can satisfy me, the only thing that has any meaning at all. My life, interior and exterior, is the result of that divine operation which I must accept as it is given, and not interfere with it. That is the principle that should guide all my actions and desires. My limitations make me fail constantly in my relationship with God, but nothing that I do can influence God's love for me; it doesn't suffer from my failures at all.

Such a union of abandonment is only possible through surrender to His will and humble acceptance of His providence. In this life of seeking and serving God, so much is mysterious. However, conscience, intuition, inspiration, and other delicate movements in the soul help us discern the intricate, yet simple and unfailing desire to communicate with God who loves us unconditionally.

℣. *If God is for us, who can be against us?*

℟. *He who did not spare his own Son but handed him over for us all, how will he not also give us everything else along with him?*

Our Father …

Nine Hail Mary's, in honor of the years that Walter Ciszek spent in the camps

Glory be …

Intercessory Prayer (see page 87)

Novena III

IN A TIME OF
LOSS OR GRIEF

*You set a table before me in
   front of my enemies;*

*You anoint my head with oil;
   my cup overflows.*

*Indeed, goodness and mercy will
   pursue me all the days of my life;*

*I will dwell in the house of the Lord
   for endless days.*

—PSALM 23:5-6

Rehabilitated by
Nikolai Getman
See page 138 for
more information.

DAY ONE
Free to Serve

Daily Offering (see page 87)

In April 1955, I was liberated from the work camp and given a "restricted certificate" that limited my freedom to live and move freely in Russia. Wherever I found a residence, I had to report to the police and register my presence there. I decided to go to the nearby city of Norilsk and look for the Ukrainian priest, Father Viktor, whom I had met in the camp, and who had been released a few months earlier.

I found him living in a shanty town out on the edge of the city, together with another priest, Father Neron, also a former prisoner. There was hardly any space for me in their shed, yet they insisted that I stay with them. Spreading religion was unlawful, but with the changes after the death of Stalin, the soviet authorities tolerated the public celebration of Mass on a regular schedule. The occasional summons from the city council or threats from the secret police did not hinder the priests from continuing their pastoral work. After fourteen years in prisons and camps, I really welcomed the opportunity to work as a priest again.

Our "chapel," big enough for forty people, attracted people from all over Norilsk. They attended our services, had their children baptized, and wanted their homes blessed. We provided the sick with the sacraments and prayed the Office for the Dead. The people gave us generous offerings, convinced that faith demands some form of sacrifice. My fellow priests entrusted the ministry to these Russian faithful to me.

℣. *Do not worry about your life, what you will eat or drink, or about your body, what you will wear.*

℞. *Seek first the kingdom of God and his righteousness, and all these things will be given you besides.*

Our Father …

Eight Hail Mary's, in honor of the years that Walter Ciszek spent in Siberian cities

Glory be …

Intercessory Prayer (see page 87)

DAY TWO

Finding God

Daily Offering (see page 87)

Once I had found a regular job in a metal-refining factory and a room of my own to live, I could start organizing my priestly work. Eight hundred baptisms a year, sick calls, and other pastoral visits kept the three of us occupied day and night.

During these busy years, I learned how to balance prayer and work. Much of my prayer was reflection, which became a loving communication with God. It influenced my whole attitude and freed me to be less cautious and formal, more open and spontaneous. I realized the asceticism of my early priestly formation had become an obstacle for my apostolic zeal. It didn't matter anymore whom I met, what I ate or drank, how much time I slept, what danger awaited me, who came to visit me, what people said, what the police planned against me. Whatever happened, I accepted it as it came. The only thing that mattered was that I found God in what I did. My shortcomings, failures, and sins too, I brought to Him in humility and trust. Good or bad — nothing could divert me from God.

I meditated and said my prayers on my way

to or from work, or during dinner break. The principle I followed was to do first and then consider; whatever life brought was the subject matter of my reflections. Even when my pastoral duties kept me busy through the night until five a.m., I had no problem rising early to meditate on the spiritual value of my experiences.

℣. *Do not worry about your life, what you will eat or drink, or about your body, what you will wear.*

℟. *Seek first the kingdom of God and his righteousness, and all these things will be given you besides.*

Our Father …

Eight Hail Mary's, in honor of the years that Walter Ciszek spent in Siberian cities

Glory be …

Intercessory Prayer (see page 87)

DAY THREE
Threatened

Daily Offering (see page 87)

Periodically, the consolation my pastoral work provided would be dampened by the secret police calling me to their quarters. The officials in charge knew all about my activities and told me to stop evangelizing and interfering with soviet society and the education of the people. If not, they would send me to the camps again. Disturbed, I first kept silent when asked to stop my priestly activity. But when their pressure continued, I simply told them I would never turn away people who had come to me willingly.

After a period of silence, in the summer of 1957, the secret police approached me with a new scheme — that I work for them as pastor of an independent Roman Catholic Church they would build for me. Their plans were so outrageous that I was hardly able to contain myself. Through confessions, counseling sessions, and other meetings with parishioners, I would be expected to gather information for the government. I told the officer that he was mistaken, and I would never agree, but he insisted that I go home and consider their proposal.

People continued to request my services almost every day. They didn't know what difficulties my priestly ministry caused me. In spite of the sharp control exercised by the secret police, I welcomed all people who turned to me for assistance and did everything I could for them. No matter how much I mentally rebelled against a regime that forbade its citizens the free exercise of their religion, I had to endure it patiently.

℣. *Do not worry about your life, what you will eat or drink, or about your body, what you will wear.*

℟. *Seek first the kingdom of God and his righteousness, and all these things will be given you besides.*

Our Father …

Eight Hail Mary's, in honor of the years that Walter Ciszek spent in Siberian cities

Glory be …

Intercessory Prayer (see page 87)

DAY FOUR

Zeal

Daily Offering (see page 87)

In 1958, after my two fellow priests had left Norilsk, the people themselves who attended our small chapel now arranged for the great celebration of Easter. Months in advance, plans regarding services, confessions, and the blessing of homes and food were made. Secret committees were organized for this difficult and dangerous work.

I fully consented to their plan, including all the consequences that might result from it. I was able to stay home from work for six days and devote myself to my "parish" from early morning to late at night, giving my all to make this Easter feast a success. People were so enthusiastic about the preparations that the word spread and attracted support from all over the city. No one really understood why the city police allowed the Easter week services to be celebrated. Whatever the reason, it gave the people a unique opportunity to express their religious feelings as never before. Personally, I knew the truth and recognized God's grace at work in this celebration. I was so absorbed by the Easter liturgy that I didn't even consider threat or danger.

I felt the human spirit empowered and inflamed by the grace of the Holy Spirit.

Zeal is a state of soul inspired by God himself. I felt transformed by the divine touch; grace, the higher motivating power, did wonders in my soul. Just as God is limitless, so the soul inspired by Him feels free to act without limit. This is the miracle wrought in the souls of true apostles: God's power manifest in his chosen and inspired people.

℣. *Do not worry about your life, what you will eat or drink, or about your body, what you will wear.*

℟. *Seek first the kingdom of God and his righteousness, and all these things will be given you besides.*

Our Father …

Eight Hail Mary's, in honor of the years that Walter Ciszek spent in Siberian cities

Glory be …

Intercessory Prayer (see page 87)

DAY FIVE
Easter Joy

Daily Offering (see page 87)

The midnight Easter mass attracted hundreds to our chapel. The glory of the Risen Christ reflected itself in the people who stood for four hours and more. The atmosphere in and around the overcrowded chapel was one of boundless joy, expressed in the continuous singing. The cold or the danger of arrest, with the police watching outside, did not prevent the people from participating in the services. Many waited for hours to enter the small chapel to pray and to have food baskets blessed.

No human power could have produced a devotion as witnessed that Easter midnight of 1958. Touched by the grace of God, the faithful praised Him with their whole being. Enthusiasm can create strong feelings, but when it remains on the human level, it cannot compare with the feeling of being in direct contact with God. The difference can be felt, but not adequately explained. It's a mystery, deeply rooted in the heart and soul of human life.

The celebration of the following three Easter days filled my soul with untold joy and peace. These days were a recompense for my past years in prison.

I spiritually sensed and felt the presence of God in my whole being — an experience unequaled before or after this occasion. It confirmed in me God's gift of grace, how it penetrates and transforms nature, totally independent of the person receiving it. The fruit of such a God-given experience is spiritual courage.

℣. *Do not worry about your life, what you will eat or drink, or about your body, what you will wear.*

℟. *Seek first the kingdom of God and his righteousness, and all these things will be given you besides.*

Our Father …

Eight Hail Mary's, in honor of the years that Walter Ciszek spent in Siberian cities

Glory be …

Intercessory Prayer (see page 87)

DAY SIX
Arrested Again

Daily Offering (see page 87)

When I returned to work after the Easter holidays, I was arrested at the factory by a security agent who asked my name, and then quickly took me away. It caught me unaware, even though the last couple of days I had sensed some danger ahead. I thought it would be trouble with my boss after my six-day absence, but not a confrontation with the secret police.

Arrests in Russia are well planned. In a moment's notice, the culprit or suspect is apprehended and taken to an unknown location. What is happening? Why? Nobody knows. Such arbitrary deprivation of liberty, such deceitful charges should not exist in any civilized country. But who can stop such abuse of power by state officials who are driven by some false ideology and not by the common good and the needs of the people? It hurts deeply to be the victim of such injustice. Resisting is useless — you only risk being punished even more severely — and so I accepted the situation as it came. It was the only sensible thing to do. But I will never forget the experience, the dark consequence of a totalitarian regime with no justice; using only indoctrination and threats.

There was hardly time to say goodbye to my co-workers while I was led out by the security agent. They looked scared, wondering what it was all about. I got into a jeep waiting outside for me and was driven straight to the secret police headquarters in the newly built section of Norilsk.

℣. *Do not worry about your life, what you will eat or drink, or about your body, what you will wear.*

℟. *Seek first the kingdom of God and his righteousness, and all these things will be given you besides.*

Our Father …

Eight Hail Mary's, in honor of the years that Walter Ciszek spent in Siberian cities

Glory be …

Intercessory Prayer (see page 87)

DAY SEVEN
Silent Response

Daily Offering (see page 87)

In the police headquarters, the officer in charge met me standing behind his desk, leaning on his hands. As I approached his desk, he looked at me sternly without saying a word. I, too, had no fear of him and looked him straight in the eye. Detesting my stare, he curtly said they had enough of my missionary work in Norilsk, pointed to the door, and told me to leave. I remained calm as two security guards led me out quickly, restraining myself from giving some harsh response in return.

In an adjacent office, a security man informed me that I had to be out of the city within ten days. The small shack where I lived had been confiscated. He waited for me to object, but I said nothing. He then told me to buy a plane ticket for the capital, Krasnoyarsk, and report to the secret police in that city. I was strictly forbidden to do anything in the way of religious work among the people. Again, he waited for me to comment or object. Again, I said nothing.

It took much time and patience to obtain the signatures of my various supervisors. From time to time, the security agent came to visit me and inquire how things were progressing. To move things along faster, he would assist me wherever needed. I hadn't been able to purchase a plane ticket, but the secret police had it within hours. For them, there was no such thing as a full airplane.

℟. *Do not worry about your life, what you will eat or drink, or about your body, what you will wear.*

℣. *Seek first the kingdom of God and his righteousness, and all these things will be given you besides.*

Our Father …

Eight Hail Mary's, in honor of the years that Walter Ciszek spent in Siberian cities

Glory be …

Intercessory Prayer (see page 87)

DAY EIGHT
Lamentations

Daily Offering (see page 87)

The news that the secret police had ordered me to leave Norilsk spread fast and wide. At the factory, most of my co-workers showed their sympathy when saying goodbye; others, though, kept their distance, to avoid trouble. My "parishioners" were stricken most by my departure. Fearing the secret police, many of them did not come and see me off, but sent their best wishes through others.

During these ten days, I visited many families and people. Three years of pastoral work in Norilsk had brought me in contact with many Orthodox, Ukrainians, Russians, and other nationalities. The Orthodox families who tried to get permission from Moscow for me to stay permanently in Norilsk as their acting priest were terribly disappointed. Everybody lamented that the only priest available in the city to help them spiritually had to leave. Their simple faith and devotion to the Church showed how deeply they understood the gift of God in the priesthood. More than any others, these faithful believers deeply appreciated this gift of God, and recognized the special grace given to them through this ministry. Despite the warning I'd been given, I celebrated Mass every day until I left, heard confessions, baptized, and visited the sick.

The high spiritual quality of my parishioners touched me deeply and wounded my heart. I was pained and upset that I had to part with them. Why did God not interfere and permit me to stay longer in the city to serve the people in their religious needs? He could do it so easily.

℣. *Do not worry about your life, what you will eat or drink, or about your body, what you will wear.*

℟. *Seek first the kingdom of God and his righteousness, and all these things will be given you besides.*

Our Father …

Eight Hail Mary's, in honor of the years that Walter Ciszek spent in Siberian cities

Glory be …

Intercessory Prayer (see page 87)

DAY NINE
Hope

Daily Offering(see page 87)

In these three years, my spiritual life had developed. Finding God, feeling his presence, sensing his providential care — all of this was reflected in serving people with more than obligatory, formal prayer. I became one with them in the liturgy, sacraments, and a living faith. Their spiritual needs were mine, and what I possessed spiritually, I fully shared with them, which enriched me, too. Parting from them affected my heart, mind, and spirit.

Finally, the day of departure arrived. I celebrated Mass for the last time in Norilsk and said farewell to my parishioners. Then the security agent came with his driver to take me and my luggage to the airport. The wife of the choir master accompanied me. I admired her courage. The agent had allowed her to come along, showing some humanity. When he left the airport after having arranged my flight, she took the bus back to town.

The long wait at the airport Nadezhda (Hope) drained me. When the plane finally arrived, a cold arctic morning had broken. I was helped up the ramp to the plane, because I had trouble with my knees. I had never flown before, and I was scared as the plane took off, but I was even more conscious of an uneasiness deep inside me. I thought of the people I was leaving behind and of the injustice done to me. What would the future have in store for me? God knew what He was doing, I thought, and I kept repeating "Thy will be done," but it was hard to understand. The plane flew south.

℣. *Do not worry about your life, what you will eat or drink, or about your body, what you will wear.*

℟. *Seek first the kingdom of God and his righteousness, and all these things will be given you besides.*

Our Father …

Eight Hail Mary's, in honor of the years that Walter Ciszek spent in Siberian cities

Glory be …

Intercessory Prayer (see page 87)

Magadan Hills by Nikolai Getman
See page 139 for more information.

Common Prayers

O God, I offer you all the prayers, works, joys, and sufferings of this day. Grant that I may accept unquestionably and respond lovingly to all the situations of the day as truly sent by you. May my offering win your grace, especially for the intention of this novena.

INTERCESSORY PRAYER I

Gracious God, in Russia you led Father Walter Ciszek to a deep understanding of life and of your love. Then, you brought him safely home, so that he might teach us how to abandon ourselves to your Providence. Through his intercession, hear our prayer (*pause and mention request*) and help us to do always and in everything your holy will. Amen.

---

1 Based on the Morning Offering of the Apostleship of Prayer. Cf. *He Leadeth Me*, 39, 141.

INTERCESSORY PRAYER II

Almighty God, we love, adore and praise you as our Creator and Loving Father.

Look with compassion and mercy upon us. Hear our prayer in this time of special need, and through the intercession of Father Walter Ciszek, grant the following favor if it is your Holy Will. (*pause and mention request*)

Most loving God, accept our gratitude for hearing this prayer. May the virtues and holiness of Father Walter be recognized and provide a lasting example for sinners to be reconciled and for all to grow in sanctity. For you are our God and we are your people and we glorify You, Father, Son and Holy Spirit, now and ever and forever. Amen.

FIRST PRINCIPLE AND FOUNDATION

(ST IGNATIUS OF LOYOLA)

Man is created to praise, reverence, and serve God our Lord, and by this means to save his soul. The other things on the face of the earth are created for man to help him attaining the end for which he is created.

Hence, man is to make use of them insofar as they help him in the attainment of his end, and he must rid himself of them insofar as they prove a

hindrance to him. Therefore, we must make ourselves indifferent to all created things.

A METHOD FOR REAL HEALING

(WALTER CISZEK, SJ)

Take the negative reaction, sin, disturbance of
mind (or the positive feeling), and offer it up to
the Will of God for those always in dire need of acts
of compassion. Make a simple act of surrender, and
then go on to what comes next in your life, in the
natural order of things. The moment that you feel
any disturbance, any aggravation, any break with
the Lord or a loss of peace, turn immediately to the
Spirit of Christ, and intensify your prayer. Do not
dwell on the negative, but allow the negative to be
replaced by charity, compassion, and alms-giving.

Giving in the spiritual life means giving up to
God what these people need for salvation. In this
is real healing. The whole secret is never to lose
the contact of doing God's will. In a spirit of sacrifice and suffering, you find your true self in living for others. Erase yourself totally; let Him take
over. Surrender to God, and He will do everything
for you.

SUSCIPE
(ST IGNATIUS OF LOYOLA)

Take, Lord, and receive all my liberty,
my memory, my understanding,
and my entire will,
All I have and call my own.
You have given all to me.
To you, Lord, I return it.
Everything is yours; do with it what you will.
Give me only your love and your grace,
that is enough for me. Amen

PRAYER FOR GENEROSITY

Lord Jesus, teach me to be generous;
teach me to serve you as you deserve,
to give and not to count the cost,
to fight and not to heed the wounds,
to toil and not to seek for rest,
to labor and not to seek reward,
except that of knowing that I do your will.
Amen.

PRAYER OF SURRENDER

Lord, Jesus Christ, I ask the grace to accept the sadness in my heart, as your will for me, in this moment. I offer it up, in union with your sufferings, for those who are in deepest need of your redeeming grace. I surrender myself to your Father's will, and I ask you to help me to move on to the next task that you have set for me.

Spirit of Christ, help me to enter into a deeper union with you. Lead me away from dwelling on the hurt I feel:

to thoughts of charity for those who need my love,

to thoughts of compassion for those who need my care, and

to thoughts of giving to those who need my help.

As I give myself to you, help me to provide for the salvation of those who come to me in need.

May I find my healing in this giving.

May I always accept God's will.

May I find my true self by living for others in a spirit of sacrifice and suffering.

May I die more fully to myself, and live more fully in you.

As I seek to surrender to the Father's will, may I come to trust that he will do everything for me. Amen

PRAYER FOR THE CANONIZATION
OF FATHER WALTER CISZEK, SJ

We adore you, Most Holy Trinity, and we thank you for the exemplary life of your Servant, Father Walter Ciszek.

We pray that his strong faith in your loving Providence, his great love for you, and his kindness to all people be recognized by the Church. If it be your Will, may he be given to us as a saintly model of these virtues, so that we too may be better motivated to dedicate our lives to your greater glory. We commend our petition through the prayers of the Holy Mother of God.

For to you, Father, Son, and Holy Spirit, is due all glory, honor, and worship, now and forever. Amen.

Father Ciszek is met at Idlewild Airport
(now JFK International) by his sisters
Helen and Sister Evangeline

Appendix

**SISTER ROSEMARY'S MEMORIES
OF FATHER WALTER**

written between 1987 and 1992

VIVID MEMORIES

The first time I saw Father Walter he had just returned from Russia and he visited the convent in
Reading, PA to see his two sisters. He was a small,
slight man, very different from what I expected.
Although I didn't speak to him, I noticed that he
seemed shy, unassuming and ordinary. He gave a
conference to the sisters, but I don't remember one
single word. I was a temporary professed sister at
the time and knew very little about him or his in-
credible story.

What remains very vivid, however, is the memory of Father Walter offering Mass the next morning in our Chapel. What impressed me was not his piety or appearance of great holiness, but rather something quite different. He seemed so secretive about every action. The blessing was hardly more than a slight wave of the hand, and he moved in a way that you hardly detected any motion. He was fast and very quiet during the prayers. At the consecration, he barely raised the host and the chalice. I think he was so accustomed to being vigilant and watchful celebrating Mass in Russia where he was forbidden to function as a priest, he seemed not to realize he was home free. In spite of this, I felt that he was completely absorbed in the beauty and mystery of the liturgy.

I remember his face as friendly but serious, the result of very difficult experiences that made him appear very wise. His voice seemed too soft, as if it had lost its strength from being unused in captivity. He had a great laugh, and when he smiled, he lit up the room. He was memorable, and we all talked about him a long time after he left. At that time, I never dreamed I would be writing to him in the future, or that we would meet through a spiritual connection.

LIFTING THEM TO GOD

I find it interesting that my mother knew him long before I did, and I wasn't aware of this. She was a friend of Sister Evangeline, his sister who was a Bernardine, and she wrote to him almost as soon as he returned from Russia. She often mentioned how much peace and consolation this gave her. She wrote to him about all her children, so Father knew of me before he really knew me. And even after I wrote, I guess he just accepted me as part of the large growing circle of people he loved and cared for — always expanding until it seemed to include more people than one small man could possibly include in his communications. And so he did the only thing he could — he commended them all to God. I know he often wrote down the names of those he met who asked for prayers. He kept lists of names and read them prayerfully, maybe every day. At the end, he prayed continuously, ceaselessly for these souls, lifting them to God at every Mass, in every action done for the Lord, in every prayer. His very breath, by now so labored at times, became a prayer — and he became all things to all men.

THE SUMMER OF 1970

In the beginning, I looked to Father Walter for advice only in a crisis. My first letter was a request for a Mass after my father died in 1969. I asked my superior for the stipend and she suggested sending it to Father Walter. I said okay, even though I really didn't know him. She gave me his address, and I wrote a little note and sent it off. I never expected an answer. I was completely surprised that he wrote back. I received the first letter written on May 11 — Mother's Day. I remember asking him to pray for my mother in my note, because I knew how hard it was for her to adjust to life without my father. I shared what she was going through. His response was short, but spiritually uplifting. I saved it and read it over very often. In later years, May 11 came to be a very significant date — with consolations as well as trials.

THE HEART OF THE MATTER

In 1973, when I began graduate studies and was assigned to the faculty of Alvernia College, I felt called to begin spiritual direction with Father Walter. It was a beautiful day in October when I drove up to the Jesuit Spiritual Center in Wernersville, PA to meet him. He had just finished directing a retreat and was making his own. I had called him earlier, even though he was on retreat, and asked if I might come to see him. As usual, he sounded delighted, as if that was exactly what he had been hoping for. He always made a person feel special.

At first, I never really knew what to say to him. I felt speechless and tongue-tied in his presence. But later, I just felt so keenly interested in what he had to say that I didn't even bother to speak. Just to look at him and listen was enough for me. As for Father Walter, he was just so free and unselfconscious. He never took notice of my helplessness, or if he did, he never let me know. His conversation was never light talk, but rich with substance. He went right to the heart of the matter; the small pleasantries that surround and decorate a dialogue were utterly unknown to him. At times he could be make you laugh, and then keep you captivated with stories of his experiences. He could also talk in circles about something that he struggled to explain. But all the while, in every word and gesture, you felt surrounded by his love, his true affection, his wisdom.

His conversations were always centered on what his listener asked or needed. He spoke simply of life, suffering, scripture, Mary, and God — the basics of faith. He could explain things clearly, and yet he never "had all the answers." His speech was so humble, so unassuming. He made fun of his littleness, his poor health, his simple ways, in such a way that he invited you to share the fun of this poor sorry condition — and see in yourself a shadow of the same. He could pass from fun to serious business in the blink of an eye, understanding the essence of your thought, and speaking to your heart with intuitive wisdom. He had the gift of discernment, especially in the sacrament of reconciliation, and the gift to read hearts.

COURAGE

I don't think Father Walter ever said these words to me, but he expressed this idea often: "Have the courage to stick to your schedule." When I visited him, I saw what he meant, watching him move with serenity, attending to every task with peaceful fidelity. He gave himself completely to what the day required. If it was action, he was ready. If it was peaceful contemplation, he was grateful. He had a kind of moral courage, a virtuous dedication that kept him on course. His grueling years in Russia tested him severely, but his stamina and faith kept him strong. He lived each day the best he could, in captivity as well as in freedom. When he returned to America, writing two books, giving hundreds of retreats, corresponding with close to 1,000 people, in failing health and unshared interior suffering, he still had the courage to stick to his daily schedule. His day was a prayer. There were never interruptions, only opportunities to share God's love with those who asked. If his sleep was interrupted, "that's the way God wanted it". And crowning it all was his smile — genuine, sometimes with a little joke, the perfect balance of a man at peace with all men, and at peace with God.

GOD'S GIFT TO ME

I didn't see Father Walter again for a long time - two or three years. In fact, I only wrote to him once or twice a year, at one point only after two years. He just finished *He Leadeth Me* about the same time I picked up the correspondence, at the beginning of 1973. I remember that in one letter he wrote: "I wondered what happened to you." He always encouraged me to write, as if it was something he anticipated and expected. He made me feel that my writing to him was very important — in the plan of God and not to be taken lightly.

At that time I was indecisive about a direction in my life and I sat down and wrote out the whole story. He responded immediately, a lengthy letter of great depth and affection. He took great pains and much time to answer all I asked of him, and I felt very unworthy of such a generous person. I thanked him for his support and encouragement.

A few months later, on October 4, 1973, I had an opportunity to visit him while he was making his annual retreat at the Jesuit Center in Wernersville. I asked him to be my spiritual director, and he was not at all surprised. He said that from the beginning he knew this would happen. I gave him my spiritual journal to read and began a correspondence that continued until he died. Sometimes I wrote him several letters a month, and for several years, before his correspondence grew voluminous, he answered every letter. I can't imagine how I would have persisted without him. He was God's gift to me at a time when I needed it most. At that time, I don't think I really knew the depth and blessing of this gift.

FAITH, PRAYER, LOVE

If I were asked to identify three prominent themes in Father Walter's life, they would be faith, prayer, and love.

His faith was extraordinary, even from early childhood. His mother instilled in him a strong religious spirit that helped to nurture a conscience anchored in God. Religion was a family priority, and he believed that his early formative years in the Catholic faith sustained him during his worst years in Russia. Upon his return home, faith became the basis for all his retreats, conferences, and spiritual direction. "See everything with the eyes of faith" became his mantra. It was not merely an intellectual idea, but a total surrender and acceptance, in his heart and will, of all God sent to him daily — the good, the difficult, the joys and the sufferings. He believed that God directed his life, every minute of it, and that was enough to restore his peace.

Father Walter also knew that faith could not exist without prayer. His prayer was simply a sustained relationship with God, ongoing, faithful, permeating every act and thought of each day. He loved the formal prayer of the Church, the breviary, especially the Mass — the central point of his day. I knew he began each day with prayer, and after a tiring day that ended late in the night, he would tell me that he prayed the rosary, sometimes watching a ballgame with the volume turned down saying, "I have to keep an eye on those Yankees!"

At the end he was directed by love, for God and others through his daily life of sacrifice. It was never "what I want" but always "what God wants." He often mentioned to me that to live a life of self-sacrifice is the greatest gift of love we can offer to God. Sometimes even small favors can cost so much, but for Father Walter, no call was ever an interruption, no illness was more than he could bear. There were no complaints, no looking for something better. He wanted nothing but God, and everything else was secondary. As he lived longer, he grew more loving. When he spoke to others, he sensed immediately their need for love. He was not content to only love those who were kind, but he loved especially those who did not love him or who were unlovable, humanly speaking. In this, he became a true disciple and follower of Jesus.

PRAYER WAS HIS LIFE

I know that Father Walter prayed a great deal. It was obvious from everything that he said and did. On a few occasions, more than I deserved, he shared with me the insights of his prayer and we prayed together. It was very humble and simple. He worshiped God with his whole being — mind, heart, body, and soul. He was totally at peace in prayer, perfectly unselfconscious. He seemed lost to himself, to his surroundings and to the distractions of the immediate environment. He was completely absorbed in God.

I think the first time we prayed together, it was with the breviary. He shared his book and we recited psalms by turns. He read the words slowly, with meaning, but very naturally. He spoke the words of the prayer as a jeweler might examine diamonds — with awe and reverence for the beauty of scripture. I noticed how frequently he had underlined passages and made small notes in the margins. He paused to meditate after the reading, and his labored asthmatic breath sounded like someone sleeping, but his discipline and focus proved otherwise.

He often copied lines or phrases that impressed him at prayer, and he would write these thoughts down and tape them to the lamp on his desk or table where he prayed. He would include these thoughts in his letters to people, or read them when speaking on the phone or in counseling. He took to heart every inspiration from the Holy Spirit and never let one grace slip away. He cherished these gifts from God, and gratefully treasured every grace. That is why he shared so freely what God gave, because he understood how unworthy we are to experience this intimacy with God. He moved so easily into prayer, and just as quietly it ended. It was as if the prayer never really had a beginning or an end — it was just an extension of his life. Prayer was his life.

FIDELITY TO DAILY GRACES

Part of the Jesuit Spiritual Exercises includes the practice of recording the thoughts and graces of each meditation in a spiritual notebook, to be used for prayer at a later time. These inspirations are meant to assist the soul in entering more fully into the love of God and the practice of virtue. This was Father Walter's daily custom. He never failed to write out his meditations — not just during a retreat or on a special day, but every day. He saw this practice as a way to be faithful. Fidelity to daily graces and to the routine and ordinary events of the spiritual life were of great importance to him, because if you were not faithful in these small matters, you would not have the willpower or strength in a crisis. His whole approach in this prayer was not to strain or push or become agitated: if you couldn't manage today, then maybe tomorrow; if not now, then later. God will provide a way. Take everything as it comes and don't exaggerate or become excited about any of it. The faithful, peaceful way of humble, hidden virtue is the only true path to God.

GOD-LEVEL

It is very difficult to explain how Father Walter answered questions — questions about difficulties one had in living a religious life, or the vows, or personal relationships. It's not that he couldn't answer or didn't know what to say. But I began to think that he answered the question at a level above the plane where the question was asked. He always tried to lift you out of the problem, bring you up higher, so that the way to respond to the difficulty was not from your eye level, but from God's eye level. Because of this, he often seemed to be talking about something unrelated to what you had asked. Sometimes it appeared that he didn't hear the question, or didn't really understand it. But the truth is, he heard more than what you were asking. He heard the deeper implications of your need or your hurt, your longing or suffering. He always tried to show you a deeper reality, to help you see things in the context of faith, to point the way to surrender and trust.

ACCOMMODATING TO EVERYONE

It seems to me that there was no end to the constant flow of people in Father Walter's life. I am reminded of Christ in Mark's Gospel, always being surrounded and hemmed in by the crowd. There was never a time that I visited him that he did not have visitors. Somebody was always knocking on his door, or the phone never failed to ring. I know that he was often tired, but he never turned anyone away. You had to know him well, the condition of his health, to realize that he must have been fatigued.

I only remember one time that he let the phone ring and did not answer. He said he knew who was calling. He told me it was an old, slightly confused man who kept talking in circles with no coherence. He would ring up in the middle of the night and keep him on the line for an hour. Sometimes he made sense, but most often he just argued about ridiculous things that had no end. Father never hung up on him or put him off. He responded as if the man was perfectly coherent and always tried to be kind. This particular time, we had just begun my retreat and it was late in the evening, and Father knew the prudence of not answering the phone. It struck me then how discrete he was with difficult people. Humanly speaking, he was very strong and quick to react, but it was under control and that was the difference. It's not anger, the emotion, which is the problem. It is how we let the anger influence our behavior. Jesus himself was angry, but he never did an unkind thing in his life. This was the ideal, the way Father Walter tried to live.

SURRENDER TO GOD

Whenever I would phone Father Walter or he would phone me, it was usually he who did most of the talking. It was always easier for me to talk to him in person, but on the phone I just liked to listen. He would tell me about a recent trip, or the conferences he was preparing, or some of his visitors, but then he would settle on a theme such as faith, or suffering, and he would begin to explain what this meant to him. He used examples or sometimes events from his own life, and it often appeared to be a rambling conversation. Perhaps he was only searching for words to refine an idea, to express it better, more accurately. I felt that his contemplative experiences were difficult for him to articulate, but for the sake of us who hungered to know what he knew, he struggled to put into words what we were seeking.

Several months before he died, he called and began telling me about a new way he had begun to pray. As he spoke, I began to make some notations on what he was saying, just writing phrases or words to capture significant expressions and thoughts. Later, after reading the notes, I was deeply affected by what was written. He called it a prayer, but it was not something familiar, something formal, although similar to other prayers I knew. He called it a prayer of surrender, and he tried to explain its significance in our spiritual life. I don't know if I fully understood all that he said or all that he meant to say. But from the notes I had written, I tried to connect the thoughts to explain this prayer. The words are there to point the way, but the real prayer is spoken in the heart. Each time I use this prayer, especially at times when I am upset or disturbed, I sense a powerful current of peace and calm enter my soul. No matter the difficult moment, or person, this prayer clothes me with Christ.

Take the negative reaction, sin, disturbance of mind (or the positive feeling), and offer it up to the Will of God for those always in dire need of acts of compassion. Make a simple act of surrender, and then go on to what comes next in your life, in the natural order of things. The moment that you feel any disturbance, any aggravation, any break with the Lord or a loss of peace, turn immediately to the Spirit of Christ, and intensify your prayer. Do not dwell on the negative, but allow the negative to be replaced by charity, compassion, and alms-giving.

Giving in the spiritual life means giving up to God what these people need for salvation. In this is real healing. The whole secret is never to lose the contact of doing God's will. In a spirit of sacrifice and suffering, you find your true self in living for others. Erase yourself totally; let Him take over. Surrender to God, and He will do everything for you.

BALANCE

If I were to choose another key word in the life of Father Walter, I would choose balance. He was a remarkable example of someone who knew how to keep afloat in the many storms and squalls that blow through our lives. There are many examples of this, but I always think of one in particular. Father had so many health problems: emphysema, a serious heart condition, and many complications from the long years of deprivation in Russia. He had a lot of medication that he needed to keep his physical health in line, but his illness and his sufferings never overwhelmed him. He always seemed to manage, never overly dependent on the medication or troubled by the side effects of the pills. He knew how to regulate what he ate, how much he ate, how much he slept, the medicine, the exercise, so that like a man balancing so many spinning plates, he kept an eye on each one, never neglected one for another, never let one get run down, and seemed perfectly relaxed, perfectly at ease while doing it. His life was balanced using a holistic method based on common sense and prudence.

AT MASS

I cannot say enough about the meaning of Mass for Father Walter. In the Mass he found the whole meaning of his priesthood and his life. It was the central point of his day: all hours before the Mass were a preparation, and all hours after were a thanksgiving. The Mass encompassed everything and absorbed everything, so that all things found their importance and meaning through the Mass.

At Mass, Father Walter entered into prayer beyond anything I can really explain. The mystery was that it all seemed so natural, but as the years passed, various elements of the Mass assumed greater significance for him. On several occasions I attended Mass that he offered privately, either in New York or Wernersville. In the tiny chapel, standing beside him, I felt like I was balanced on the edge of the world. The liturgy became a perfect prayer with no distractions or interruptions; it flowed like a river of calm, pure water. At the time, I remember being very peaceful and happy knowing that I shared this privileged experience with him. Every Mass is an opportunity to stand again beside Christ, and to follow the liturgy into eternity and union with God. That is what Father Walter taught me, and I am still learning.

HIGHS AND LOWS

Father Walter often spoke to me about something he called "the highs and the lows." These expressions were sometimes difficult for me to understand because they were usually based on his experiences. At first I thought he must be talking about good days and bad days. We all experience these, like a sudden high when something goes well, when we receive a compliment or good news. And we all know what it means to be brought low in life —

by others, by our own mistakes or unexpected sad news. As time went on, I heard him refer to highs and lows in other ways. He referred to sin as the ultimate low. This, he said, is what really brings us down, what really degrades us. The Cross is another low. It is a shadow across our heart bringing us the memory of Christ's sacrifice, the price he paid to redeem us. Prayer is a high, all the time, even when it is a struggle, or *seems* fruitless or burdened by distractions. Friends are a high, and the joy or peace we experience in our friendships is the Lord's gift to keep us from becoming too lonely while we wait for our eternal reunion.

Father had hundreds of ways of to explain these highs and lows, and it seemed to me that sometimes he translated every human experience of every day into one or the other. Finally, I began to realize that the highs and lows of his life were like so many beautiful graces, showered upon him at every moment. He never looked for one or the other, just as we cannot choose which drop of rain will fall upon us in a rainstorm. We are bathed in the rain, we are wet, period. So all that God sends us is meant to cover us, wrap us in the shower of his love. The extreme high, the middle high, the deepest low, the small bump, the flat fall — everything is part of this shower in life, helping us to grow in love and in holiness. That is our daily, common, and most intimate experience with the Lord.

And Father Walter was unique in still another way. He *preferred* the lows, he actually did. One time he told me that when things are going well for him, when all seems upbeat and right, and he feels happy and content, he takes a piece of paper and writes: "pain, grief, sorrow, humiliation" and puts it in his pocket. "That," he said with a chuckle, "brings me back to earth and keeps me from disaster. I trust suffering as coming from the hand of the Lord; the other, I'm not always sure about."

INSPIRATIONS

Someone once asked me if Father Walter was a charismatic, meaning "filled with the Holy Spirit." I said that there wasn't anyone I knew who was more Spirit-filled, open and alive to the divine indwelling of God. I remember how attuned he was to the words of Scripture, how he contemplated the meaning of a special prayer, or a line from a spiritual book. He was like a child, just filled with amazement and delight at what he had discovered.

These "inspirations" would come to him at any time, but mostly in prayer or at Mass. He would read something and then spend the next few weeks totally absorbed by the depth and power of this statement. In his phone conversations and letters, it became the central subject. If any visitor came, he would spend the greater portion of the visit explaining the beautiful meaning in this line, as if the visitors had come just for that purpose. And knowing his spiritual perception, perhaps he knew they had.

Father Walter was alive with the Spirit of God, and what he shared was a result of the fullness of grace and wisdom that flowed into his heart. He longed to share all he had received with others, and he never neglected or took lightly the profound effect of these graces on other souls. On this Feast of Pentecost, I think of him now, filled with the vision of God, alive in the Spirit forever.

THE MINISTRY OF LETTER-WRITING

Sometimes, at some point in my morning, I say to myself: "I wonder if I got any mail!" That seems to be everybody's high point in the day. There was a time years ago when I would anticipate, with many prayerful thoughts, receiving a letter from Father Walter. His letters were like telegrams from God — so precious and helpful. I kept them all, and now when I read them again, I am still finding help, inspiration, counsel, direction, and comfort.

Letter-writing for Father Walter was a ministry, especially in his later life. He spent hours at his desk writing letters. He never went anywhere, on vacation or on a retreat, or to help out at a mission or a parish, without taking along a packet of letters to answer. And the letter-writing was not just a quick dash of a short note. It was not a superficial little card or a mere social contact. First of all, he saw very clearly why people were writing. The bulk of his correspondence grew after he published his first book, and again after his second. People were deeply affected by what he wrote, and they needed or wanted to hear more. They felt he had a grasp of the essentials in life. He knew what was important and was very close to God. People trusted him, trusted his judgment and his counsel. *He did not preach like the Scribes and Pharisees; he taught with authority.*

Father Walter always mentioned in his writing the specific letter he had received, his gratitude for the Mass stipends, when the Mass was offered, and thanked for prayers. He was very grateful for the concerns of his many friends, amazed at their gifts and donations, and he gave himself tirelessly to each one. He re-read each letter a second or third time before answering. He continuously prayed for the many intentions recommended to him and prayed for each one by name. This personal interest and his careful response spoke to all of us so clearly of the unique and personal love God has for each soul on earth. No one is ever neglected, passed over, considered too insignificant. Father helped people to feel hopeful again. He made faith seem real. Because he cared so much, we could believe in God's love all the more. In that sense, his ministry of letter-writing was a special vocation.

He was faithful to it up to the time he died. He had almost finished his whole Christmas card project at the time of his death — over 1,000 cards — in spite of crippling arthritis, great physical exhaustion, and daily, continuous pain. He struggled to the end, even though he knew that time was running out. He was a true friend, a faithful servant of God.

THE CHILDREN'S FRIEND

Children were a special part of Father Walter's life. He was perfectly at ease with children and communicated with them kindly and directly. There was no hesitation, no awkwardness — the mark of a kind and unaffected heart. He loved children because they represented new life and the vigorous, energetic desire to grow, to be alive. He sensed in children a yearning and a hunger for truth. Often, children are innocent and not burdened by mistrust, hostility, or the problems that affect adults who have gone through stormy years. They came to him with charming reverence. They sensed his goodness and felt safe in his company. They knew he was a friend.

Hearing Father Walter speak about children gave me an insight into the gospels that highlight Jesus welcoming them with open arms, in spite of the apostles who tried to keep them quiet and apart. On one occasion, he told me about a woman who visited him for counseling, bringing her four children to the session, most likely out of necessity. He could see that the mother was very distraught, and her parenting skills needed work, but even with the distraction of having four active, somewhat noisy and very bored children needing attention from time to time, he was completely relaxed; nothing interrupted their focused, hour-long conversation. As the session ended, he prepared to say Mass for the little community. He told me that he arranged the chairs in a semi-circle, and gave the children some simple roles in the liturgy so they could feel important. This was a totally different experience for them. Up close and personal, they felt included and watchful. The Mass did not take more than twenty minutes, and his solemn, gentle spirit gave them a space to settle and absorb something new. It was an intimate and meaningful time for mother and children, a sanctuary which gave them much needed peace.

HE MADE YOU FEEL WONDERFUL

I will never forget the day Father Walter came to visit my family. It was in July of 1975. I was so excited because he would finally meet everyone I had been telling him about, all the people I had asked him to pray for so many times. Several of my aunts and uncles came for this visit, and they welcomed him like a best friend, found again. I still remember the scene as Father moved among them. I was amazed that he knew just the right approach and spoke so easily about their interests.

He knew how to communicate personally with each one. He could delight, inspire, and engage with each person on a level that was exactly and perfectly suited to their mutual conversation. He really understood human nature. He spoke to their hearts, and could tap right into the goodness, the soundness of each person's character and draw it to the surface with grace and utter respect. When he spoke to you, he gave you dignity, a kind of special recognition. You knew he listened, even if the story was poorly told. Where others lost interest, he encouraged you to go on, and with a few words you knew he understood what you meant and could offer a few thoughts that finally seemed to make sense of it all. Even if *what* he said was not entirely clear, *how* he spoke and his very presence communicated the real message. He really made you feel wonderful; it's just that simple.

HIS HANDS

I remember that sometimes when I would visit Father Walter and he would talk to me, I would find myself very conscious of his hands. They were large hands, workman's hands. They were not rough and calloused anymore because his days of hard manual labor were behind him. But in spite of the softness now, they were strong and powerful, and you could just imagine the career they had seen. The fingers were short but thick, as if they held condensed power. And I used to think that his hands matched him very well. He was small in stature, but a dynamo of energy, willpower, and courage.

I saw his hands in many positions: at prayer, holding the Eucharist, giving absolution, grasping the outstretched hand of a friend. They were an extension of himself - so expressive and so warmly human. His hands were always busy, whether he was writing (most often) or pointing to the words in his Bible as he prayed, or even wiping dishes, serving a meal, dialing a phone number. His hands were at work, and the work was a service. Sometimes I thought that his hands were like sacramentals, a source of grace extending into the world.

HUMBLE PRAYER

One time when I was talking to Father Walter, he said something which brought tears to my eyes. We were talking about the spiritual life, and he said "just to bow down your head before God in prayer is a grace; no one is worthy."In that instant, I imagined him with head bowed, lost in prayer, and I felt deeply moved by such humility and tender love before God. I sensed that this was always his attitude in prayer, and the more he prayed, the more unworthy he felt because he really understood his place in the universe, his insignificance, like Francis of Assisi who prayed: *Who are you O God, and who am I.*

I thought of my own prayer, at times so distracted and self-conscious, and I knew immediately why Father Walter was different. He who knew God so intimately, who tried so hard to do God's will, still saw himself as an unprofitable servant unworthy to be in God's presence. I was reminded of the man in the Gospel who stood at the back of the Temple, beating his breast and saying, "Lord, have mercy on me, a sinner."

It is a grace to understand how humility transforms us from within, and how it makes us more like God. I was moved by the holiness and sacredness implied in the words he used, because they drew me into the reality of what true prayer really is. "He must increase, and I must decrease." That is why we pray — to be more like God.

WITH DIGNITY

I remember visiting Father Walter in New York and noticing how he always wore a black shirt, black pants, and in a formal situation, the Roman collar. The shirt was usually the same, too. It was a type of sweater with a little pearl button at the neck. I don't know if there was more than one, but I suspect there probably wasn't. One time, I happened to see him in a good light and I couldn't believe my eyes: he was wearing a Mickey Mouse/Disney World T-shirt under the black, probably something he had received as a gift. Father never wasted anything, and this was a perfectly good shirt, just not something he wanted to wear in public. One time he told me that he had been forced to live without his blacks and Roman collar for 21 years in Russia, and he was making up for lost time. He wore his priestly attire now with dignity, something earned, like a badge of courage.

The priesthood was his gift and calling. He had fought a long, hard battle to maintain the integrity of his vocation in Russia. He could not understand why those who did not face these hardships could so easily surrender the prize. It mystified and it hurt him really, to see others so casual about their ministry. And yet he was not narrow-minded or inflexible. He was sincerely tolerant of everyone, and never gave any indication of disapproval. When asked his opinion, he was honest, non-judgmental, with the reasoned logic of a man who has searched long and hard for truth, and certain of what he believed.

BEDROOM CHAPEL

After his second heart attack, when he was limited to one floor and had to cut down on retreats, visits, speeches, and other activity, Father was given permission to reserve the Blessed Sacrament in his private bedroom. He would say Mass in this room, or at his dining room table, usually two Masses a day, something he practiced even after his health began to fail.

When I visited him once, he was showing me around his apartment and I saw that the top of his dresser was covered with a white cloth, as if set for Mass. It was an altar really, holding the chalice and paten, the stole and purificator, and a small container of wine. I understood that this was the place where he offered daily Mass. I realized then, how intimately he lived with God, here in the very place where he slept, and dressed, and prayed. And right there, in a small green file box off to one side of the altar-dresser, the God of heaven and earth was reserved. Before the file box was a small glass vigil, a little shabby looking, flickering with a burning candle day and night.

He never spoke to me about this. He never pointed to his tabernacle or explained about the Mass on the dresser, but I knew it without asking. At the time, when I looked around and realized what I was seeing, I felt drawn into his precious, sacred relationship with God. I felt it was something very personal, this privilege he had, and not to be discussed too freely, because the relationship of God with every soul is hardly public information. It was sacred in spite of being reduced to something so common and ordinary, bordering almost on the unnoticeable. And yet it was deeper, more beautiful, more purely faithful than anything I had ever known. He was bonded to God by a belief, a hope, and a charity that made everything holy. Father Walter touched God. He made contact. And he did it with a faith that never failed him.

HUMILITY

When Father Walter returned to the United States, what he knew before Russia, and what he saw after captivity was divided by a gap of 23 years. It was a huge adjustment, and the cost was overwhelming. Although he never spoke of specifics, he often implied that he struggled with difficult situations. I remember one occasion when he told me that for the first few years after his return, he felt so frustrated that he would sometimes spend a few hours in a movie theatre, watching a wild-western with lots of noise and shooting, just so he wouldn't be noticed crying!

Father Walter rarely, if ever, let anyone know all that he suffered because of failures and humiliations. It was a private affair between himself and God. Most people when they met him found him upbeat and happy. This sunny disposition was never artificial. His genuine joy concealed an interior, hidden treasure that was the foundation of his life. His meditations on humility were food for his soul. One time during a visit, he opened his bible to read to me a favorite passage of scripture: *My child, be gentle in carrying out your business, and you will be better loved than a lavish giver. The greater you are, the more humbly you should behave, and then you will find favor with the Lord. For great though the power of the Lord is, he accepts the homage of the humble. Do not try to understand things that are too difficult for you, or try to discover things that are beyond your powers. Concentrate on what has been assigned you; what you have been taught already exceeds the scope of the human mind.*[2] He read it to me slowly, line by line. Then he just smiled and nodded, as if to say: there it is, all in a nutshell; as much as you want, as much as you can accept and bear.

---

2 New Jerusalem Bible, Ecclesiasticus/Sirach 3:17-23.

COUNSELING

I know that sometimes, when people would come to Father Walter for counseling, they would not come alone. Very often, a woman would bring her children or a couple would have a baby or two. Many of these people were very poor. Maybe he had met them on the street during one of his walks, and he would strike up a conversation. People just naturally opened up to him, and he always saw their deeper need.

When they came, his first concern was their immediate needs. Were they hungry? Tired? In need of clean clothes, a hot cup of tea? He would prepare a whole meal for them, and then he would join them, so that this sharing of food became a celebration of his love and deep concern. It was in these encounters that he touched their hearts, when they relaxed and could see him at his natural best. In such openness there was no hidden agenda. When they spoke, he listened. And when they asked his advice, he presented the truth as he lived and believed it. It was always rooted in the Gospels, always the fruit of his deep, intense prayer and much suffering.

Often, after a session with someone, he would ask if the person wished to receive the Sacrament of Penance. He was very direct. It was, after all, what they came for, even if they did not consciously know it. He would frequently offer a Mass for them immediately after. These anchors, Mass and the sacraments, kept him solidly centered and authentic; they were primary in his life. Everyone would gather around the table and he would invite them into the feast that has no equal on this earth — the divine Feast of Love, receiving Jesus Christ in an intimacy that would strengthen their faltering faith. It was as if he drew away a veil and let them really see, for the first time, the length and width and height and depth of God who loved them unconditionally.

NO COMPLAINTS

I never heard Father Walter complain about anything, ever. Maybe it was because he had been deprived of everything while in prison and had been stripped down to naked, bare existence that he now had no reason to complain. If he did share some difficulty, it was usually described with a touch of humor. It never got the best of him, or disturbed his peace. "That's the way God wanted it," he would say, and he believed that as truth — that *everything* is part of God's plan. Nothing happens to us that God does not permit, or even arrange. Each suffering and inconvenience is exactly in line with his will. It is we who are so eager to change things. And when we can't, we complain. How foolish, how far from the truth, that everything is grace.

HEAR HIS VOICE AGAIN

When I would phone Father, he would usually pick up by the third ring. I often wondered if the constant stream of calls were a burden, especially at night or when his energy was depleted. But he never ignored any call; he always answered if he was home. He once told me he would even interrupt a private Mass to answer the phone, believing that each call was ordained by God.

I remember how his calls filled me with joy and I was content just to listen, especially when he shared the fruit of his prayer. His personality vibrated through the phone: the quick and easy laugh, the gentleness of his voice, the genuine concern and even tenderness for all of us whom he loved so much. Sometimes now, when I close my eyes, I can hear his voice again, the voice of one who was completely at peace with himself and humanity — that soft, slightly higher pitched voice of a man who had born more than his share of life's suffering with no regrets. It was an honor and privilege to have known him, and to call him my friend.

SAFELY HOME

My last visit with Father Walter was brief, about one month before he died. I knew it was the last time I would ever see him alive on this earth because his health was failing, and I think he knew this too. I don't remember what we talked about, but I was acutely aware of the time passing, and before long, the doorbell rang and the visit was over. A quick hug, and a final blessing, and then I was walking out the door for the trip home.

I remember how he stood on the steps and watched me go. I remember waving to him from the car as I saw him standing in the doorway of his apartment, getting smaller and smaller as we drove down the street, until finally, I couldn't see him at all. He just disappeared from my view, and a few months later, he disappeared from this earth. At the moment I was leaving him, I thought my heart would break and I could hardly keep from crying. But I was comforted to know that he would soon be with God whom he loved above all else in this world, safely home forever.

EPILOGUE (2019)

Father Walter Ciszek passed away in the Bronx, New York, on Saturday, December 8, 1984, the Feast of the Immaculate Conception. Early in the morning, the maintenance man for the Jesuits at John XXIII Ecumenical Center where he was living knew he was not well and wanted to see if he was awake. He knocked on his door, and when he failed to answer, he used his key to enter the apartment and found Father Walter sitting in his recliner chair as if sleeping, but he quickly realized that he had died.

For several months Father Walter had been getting weaker. When I spoke with him in November, he was short of breath and suffering from terrible joint pain. He told me he was using a cane because he could barely walk and had difficulty moving. The evening before he died, he made a last call to his sister Loretta and they spoke briefly, but at the end of the conversation he told her "it won't be long." The previous year, in December, he was speaking to me about his devotion to Mary, and he said that on the vigil of the Immaculate Conception earlier in the month, "he had spent the night with the Immaculate Conception." I never questioned these statements, or asked for an explanation, but they are fixed in my memory like signals — markers of these last final moments before he would no longer be with us.

I was able to attend his wake and funeral in New York, held at the Chapel of Fordham University. The day following the funeral, his sister and I were invited to return to his apartment in the Bronx before we left for Reading, so that Sister Evangeline could see the room where he died, and perhaps collect some items for the family. As I looked around the room, I noticed something I had seen so often during my visits. It was a small piece of paper taped to the lamp that sat on his dining room table — the very table where he offered his final Masses, where he sat to read scripture, pray the breviary, and where he met the many souls who came to him seeking spiritual direction. I walked to the table and leaned in to read what was written, in his own handwriting, on the paper. "Look at his place, He is not there.[3] But the humble shall own the land and enjoy the fullness of peace.[4] Surrender to God and He will do everything for you.[5]"

I am so blessed to have received so many amazing graces through my relationship with this

---

3 Cf. Matthew 28:6.
4 Psalm 37:11.
5 Cf. Psalm 37:5.

holy, humble Jesuit priest. I cannot imagine my life without this gift, for which I am forever grateful.

The Gulag Collection

The Gulag Collection is a unique collection of 50 paintings by Ukrainian artist and Gulag survivor Nikolai Getman, who spent eight years in Siberia and then worked for 40 years to create this stunning visual chronicle of the Gulag. "I undertook the task," Getman explained, "because I was convinced that it was my duty to leave behind a testimony to the fate of millions of prisoners who died and who should not be forgotten."

Born in Kharkov, Ukraine, in December 1917, Nikolai Getman began drawing at an early age and became a professional artist after graduating from the Kharkov Art College. He served with the Red Army in the Second World War and saw military action. Following his discharge in October 1945, Getman was with other artists when one of them drew a mocking picture of Stalin on a piece of cigarette paper. The whole group was quickly arrested for anti-Soviet propaganda and agitation. Getman was sentenced under Article 58 of the Criminal Code to ten years' imprisonment and five years' suppression of civil rights. He spent eight years in one of the most notorious camps of the Gulag, Kolyma, located in the Russian Far East. He was finally freed in August 1953.

From the day he was released, Getman began painting a series of pictures from memory about life and death in the Gulag. Because the Gulag was a forbidden topic, even under Stalin's successors, he had to work in secret, telling no one what he was doing, not even his wife. It was not until 1993 that the paintings were publicly exhibited in Russia. After a long illness, Nikolai Getman died in Russia in 2004, at the age of 86, but his haunting pictures of the Gulag Archipelago, the biggest and most deadly prison in the history of man, remain with us.

COVER: THE LAST OLP

Getman discovered the abandoned camp shown here while on a fishing trip long after his release. Such camps can be found throughout Siberia. At many of them the skeletal remains of deceased inhabitants are still strewn over the ground. The mounds in the background of this camp are former mining sites. The sunlight slanting from the clouds symbolizes the dawning of a new era that

Khrushchev's reforms brought—hope and freedom for the prisoners of the Gulag fortunate enough to have survived. After Stalin's personality cult was denounced in 1956 at the 20th Convention of the Soviet Communist Party, Khrushchev's "Spring Thaw" began and the "corrective camps" of the Gulag were closed down. The prisoners were released and some were rehabilitated. Leaving the prison camp, however, was usually not the end of a prisoner's problems. Many former inmates were discriminated against, for example, by being denied promotions and treated otherwise badly. The stigma of being in the Gulag hung over many of the innocent throughout their lives.

PAGE 26: IN THE NKVD'S DUNGEON

This is one of the few paintings in the collection that depicts an event or circumstance which Getman did not actually witness. It is dedicated to Aleksandr Getman, the artist's brother, who was executed on December 1, 1934—more than likely having been led down a dimly lit corridor and shot in the back, in a basement where few were likely to hear. Aleksandr Getman was among a group tried as spies and dissidents operating out of Leningrad. All the victims of this trial were later reportedly rehabilitated—that is, had their names and public standing restored. The artist is intent on seeing his brother's name restored officially and publically. His campaign to thus memorialize his brother has so far been frustrated, however, both by the Soviet government and now by the Russian government.

PAGE 46: WAITING TO BE SHOT

This painting is meant to remember a group of 159 men taken from their barracks in the middle of the night and executed by the NKVD. Such occurrences were common and often without any apparent reason. New prisoners quickly came to understand what being dragged out in the middle of the night meant. Those taken away never returned. The men in the painting are clearly aware that they are going to be killed.

PAGE 66: REHABILITATED

The man depicted is holding his rehabilitation papers, documents in which the Russian state declares him a free man with a restored name. Freedom after the Gulag, however, was often a mixed experience. Many former inmates remained under travel restrictions and could live only in certain areas. The stigma of having been a prisoner in the Gulag also made it difficult to advance professionally. The artist himself was denied promotion in his artist's union years after he had been released and Stalin's cult denounced. Many former prisoners internalized the stigma. They felt somehow different, even guilty, notwithstanding the fact that they knew they had done nothing wrong. In 1991, President Boris Yeltsin of Russia issued a decree that would provide monetary compensation for survivors of the Gulag. The former prisoners would be paid a sum prorated for the amount of time served. The lump sum which Getman received was small, approximately the same as his pension of $50 per month. When he received his rehabilitation papers, Getman personalized the original of this painting by affixing his rehabilitation documents to the man's hands.

PAGE 86: MAGADAN HILLS (GOLGOTHA)

In 1932, members of the Tsaregradsky, Bilibin and Drapkin expedition discovered gold at the mouth of the Utinny River. A settlement was built between the villages of Balaganny and Ola, the hills there destroyed, piers built, and the settlement named Magadan after a nearby stream. Forced laborers were brought in to build roads from Magadan to the gold. Building the roads was incredibly harsh labor in the permafrost. The prisoners were poorly fed and worked for long hours under fierce conditions with rudimentary tools. The sentiment expressed here is that the roads were built on human bones—that every hill, every gully, and every path in Magadan represents human lives and could be the site of a human grave. The sun is eclipsed to symbolize the darkness and evil that cast its shadow over the people of the Soviet Union. The cross represents the enormous burdens the prisoners had to bear. It also symbolizes Christ's trek up the hill of Golgotha, which the artist likens to the prisoners' journey.

Courtesy of Victims of Communism Memorial Foundation, Washington DC